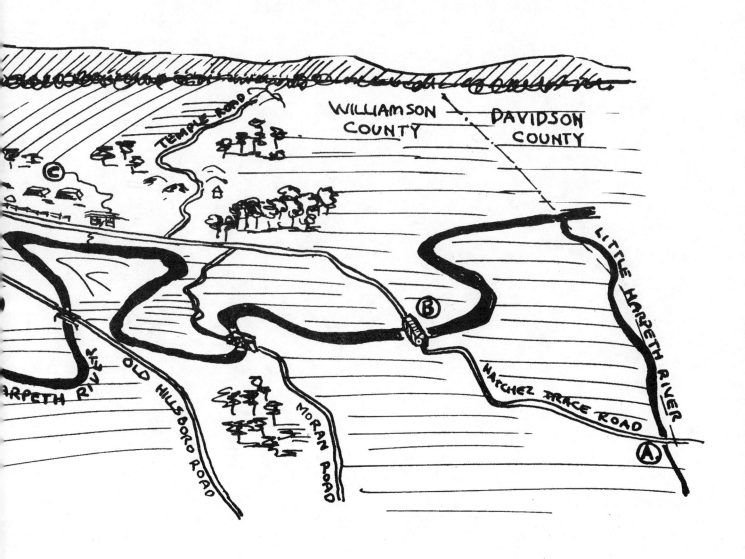

howing historic points of interest

THE HARPETH RIVER

A BIOGRAPHY

By JAMES A. CRUTCHFIELD

With Pen and Ink Drawings by the Author

The Overmountain Press
JOHNSON CITY, TENNESSEE

ISBN 1-57072-16-9
Copyright © 1972 by James A. Crutchfield
Reprinted 1994 by The Overmountain Press
Printed in the United States of America

1 2 3 4 5 6 7 8 9 0

DEDICATION

This book is dedicated to my wife,

Regena

with whom I have spent many happy

hours on the Harpeth,

and

to my mother,

Frankie

who instilled in me at an early age

my love for history.

"This family of Harpeths contains within their embrace more fine farming land than any other stream in Tennessee."

Killebrew, *Resources of Tennessee*, 1874

A NEW WORD TO THE READER

When I wrote *The Harpeth River: A Biography* in the early 1970s, I was an aspiring young writer who had never been published before. Imagine my surprise when I learned that the limited, first edition of the book had rapidly sold out and that an unlimited, second printing was forthcoming. Then imagine my further surprise when I was informed that the second printing was exhausted as well. Then, imagine my ultimate surprise in 1973, when I received notification from the American Association for State and Local History that my book had been awarded a Certificate of Commendation. By then, the publisher had gone out of business and no further printings were done.

The demand for *The Harpeth River* during its out-of-print years has been constant. Even though the counties through which the Harpeth River flows, particularly Williamson, were constantly undergoing dramatic changes during all these years and an entirely new generation of residents called the area home, the book continued to be sought out by local and regional history buffs. Library copies mysteriously disappeared, and those copies that did remain on the shelves soon became tattered and torn. For more times than I can remember, I was asked, "When is *The Harpeth River* going to be reprinted?"

Now, with eighteen books behind me and with several more in progress, imagine my pleasure when The Overmountain Press decided recently to publish a reprint of the book. Although many of the places and buildings depicted within its pages have long since disappeared and several of the people have passed on, the volume's true value now is the statement it makes to the way things were, once-upon-a-time ago, as perceived by a young man who loved the river and the land through which it flowed.

James A. Crutchfield
Franklin, Tennessee
September 1994

A WORD TO THE READER

I suppose that any author of a work dealing with as complex a subject as history should strive for a happy medium between the detail into which he would like to go and the detail which will be tolerated by the reader. There are extremes that can be cited of both cases: one where the author labors through page after page of dates, people, and events which once read are forgotten; the other where the facts are so sparse that the work is hardly more than an introduction.

If this book is guilty of either of these extremes, it will be the latter. Hopefully, however, I have presented more than a cursory history of the Harpeth River Valley. Granted, there are gaps in this history, and certainly there are events and historic occasions not mentioned in this book that are a vital part of the Valley's heritage. However, I think that probably the finest tribute that can be given a book is that it instills enough interest in the reader to encourage him to delve even more deeply into the subject matter by further reading or on-site inspection of the material covered.

It is my desire that this little book will serve as such a stimulus to those interested readers who love this river and its land, and who would like to learn more about the background of the places that they are familiar with, and of the people who loved this same river and this same land in years gone by.

Even though the Harpeth River has its beginnings as an insignificant stream in Rutherford County, and collects its waters from Rutherford, Williamson, Davidson, Cheatham, and Dickson Counties, the river really belongs to Williamson and Cheatham Counties. Rutherford County has the Stones River and its tributary system to drain it, while Dickson County is carved by tributaries of three major river systems: the Cumberland, the Duck, and the Harpeth. Practically all of Davidson County's water flows either directly or through numerous creeks into the Cumberland. The only exceptions occur in the extreme southwestern corner of the county, where the Harpeth system drains a fertile farm land.

Williamson County, on the other hand, is almost entirely dependent on the Harpeth and its tributaries for its drainage. There are a few streams which have their beginnings in the southern part of the county and which flow into the Duck River. This Duck River watershed is insignificant, however, when compared to that area serviced by the Harpeth.

While Cheatham County, through which the Cumberland River flows, is not as dependent on the Harpeth as is Williamson, significant southern and western portions of the county do depend on the Harpeth for their drainage.

If the history contained in the following pages is slanted toward Cheatham and, to an even greater degree, toward Williamson County, the reason for this comes from their greater dependence on the Harpeth.

In writing this book I have related facts that have been picked up by me at random over the years. I am grateful to many people, however, for the knowledge they have shared with me which has allowed me to expand upon these facts. Specifically, I would like to thank L. N. Greer, Miss Sonja Overby, Mrs. Joe Bowman, W. P. Bruce, Sr., Wendell King, Sr., Wendell King, Jr., W. R. Wills, II, Albert Ganier, Sr., Mrs. Sam Woolwine, Mrs. Hugh Channell, Mrs. Livingfield More, Colonel Campbell Brown, Miss Ruby Primm, Bob McGaw, Bob McBride and I. C. Simpkins for sharing with me details of this history that were familiar to them. I would be quick to add, however, that I am totally responsible for the interpretation of their knowledge, and any errors made in this interpretation are mine alone. I would also like to express my thanks for the use of the facilities of the Tennessee State Library in Nashville. And finally, to Mrs. Paulette Coleman, who performed all of the typing and manuscript preparation, I offer many, many thanks.

One additional word is in order. In many places throughout the text I have used the names Harpeth and Big Harpeth interchangeably. This grows out of my habit of using the names synonomously. They refer to the same river; the prefix "Big" is used in some cases to distinguish more readily between it and one of the other "Harpeth" rivers.

JAMES A. CRUTCHFIELD

March, 1972
Nashville, Tennessee

CONTENTS

LIST OF ILLUSTRATIONS

INTRODUCTION

Rivers have always held a certain amount of fascination for mankind. Maybe it is because the valleys of many rivers served as the birth places of civilization—places where the very first activities took place that could honestly be called urban development. Man apparently has always liked to settle beside rivers, possibly because of the transportation that streams afford, and in the cases of the larger rivers, because of the annual flooding and resulting renewal of the soil brought about each spring.

We have all read of the importance of the Nile River to ancient Egypt. We know by looking at a map of the Near East that the Fertile Cresent was that area defined by two rivers, the Tigris and the Euphrates. Less known at one time, but now fully documented, are the histories of the ancient cities that evolved on the Indus River in India. Of course, the Tigris, the Euphrates and the Indus were and still are large rivers, serving multiple purposes. As already mentioned, they are readily available for transportation and shipping, carry rich soil brought down from the highlands every spring, and also serve as a source of irrigation in dry weather.

In our own country, rivers have served just as importantly as places to settle by and as a means of transportation. Practically every large city in the United States is on the banks of a fairly large river. New York is at the confluence of the Hudson and the East, Washington is on the Potomac, New Orleans is near the mouth of the Mississippi, St. Louis and Memphis are on the banks of the Mississippi, and the list could go on and on.

Rivers, too, in the United States have served as vehicles for exploration. Henry Hudson explored the Hudson, La Salle sailed down the Mississippi, and Lewis and Clark used the Missouri as their highway for exploration of the Louisiana Territory. In a more local vein, John Donelson and his hearty assemblage aboard the flagship "Adventure" and its sister boats sailed from Fort Patrick Henry down the Holston and the Tennessee to the Ohio, up the Ohio to the Cumberland, and up the Cumberland to the Bluffs where they joined James Robertson's overland party at the site that would one day become known as Nashville. While this voyage was planned and could not be called pure exploration, I suspect that, since the route was largely uncharted at the time, the trip turned out to be a joint exploration and settlement party.

Just as rivers have served as a source of wonderment for men of all eras, the need to write about them has provided an equally strong attachment. Alan Moorehead has done a masterful job in describing both branches of the Nile in his books, *The White Nile* and *The Blue Nile*. Likewise, Emil Ludwig has treated the same river with true historical professionalism in his book, *The Nile*. I guess just about everyone at one time or another has read Mark Twain's treatise, *Life on the Mississippi*, concerning that mighty river which separates east from west in our own country. The National Geographic Society has recently produced three beautiful books, with excellent color photographs—one of the Nile, another on the Amazon, and the latest on the Mississippi. We can read about John Wesley Powell's treacherous journey down the Colorado in a recently published book, released to celebrate the 100th anniversary of that famous trip.

There are some beautifully written books in the "Rivers of America" series published by Rinehart. This series covers many of the more celebrated rivers in the country. One of the more interesting ones is *The Tennessee*, by the late Donald Davidson. This book, published in two volumes, records the history of the Tennessee River from earliest times on down to when the volumes were written in 1946-48. An equally interesting book, however, one that confines itself to a single aspect of the river, is *Steamboatin' on the Cumberland*, by the late Byrd Douglas.

The aforementioned examples are only a small sampling of the many, many books that have been written regarding the history and times of our beloved rivers. Notably missing from among these titles and the many others that could be cited are written works about the small rivers of our country. There are reasons for this, I suspect; one being that small rivers by their very nature are not widely known to the public outside of their own areas. A book about such a river would naturally quote place-names, instances in history, and other facets of the river's background that, because of the very unfamiliarity of the reader to the area, would make for dull reading indeed. Another reason for the absence of many such books is the generalization that the smaller the river is, the less amount of history that can be told about it.

I feel, however, that there is a place on our bookshelves for works that deal with the background and history of these small, but beloved, rivers. I believe that such rivers deserve from authors just as much curiosity, professionalism, and care as would be used in volumes on the Ohio, or the Missouri, or any of the other larger rivers of America. Middle Tennessee alone has several small rivers that have their own interesting stories to tell to the public, if someone would take the time to gather these stories and put them down on paper; and if only the public would take the time to read them. Many of the tales that can be told of these rivers—among them the Elk, the Duck, the Stones, and the Buffalo —are fast disappearing because many of these stories are unpublished and have simply been passed down from generation to generation by word of mouth. History remembered in this fashion is soon forgotten. If you don't believe this statement, sit down and write the names and birthdates of your great-grandparents. Then, try to think where each one of them was born and what each man did for a living. If you are lost by this time, don't feel bad, because just about everyone else is in the same predicament. The reason for this situation, of course, lies simply in the fact that most families today do not keep proper records of births, deaths, etc. for their future generations. In this same fashion, many of the fine homes and their histories, many of the old bridges, and most of the people are forgotten. Every year finds more and more of the homes and bridges coming down and more and more of the older folks, who remember back when, passing on.

The Harpeth River and its tributary system is one of these forgotten rivers. From its humble beginnings in Rutherford County to the point some 117 miles away where it dumps its silt-laden waters into the Cumberland River below Ashland City, the Harpeth is truly a river of history, and one about which much could be written. Serving a watershed of some half-million acres, and running in and out of five Middle Tennessee counties in doing so, the Harpeth is even more impressive in its history than in its physical attributes.

The Harpeth Valley was at one time the home of many thousands of Mound Building Indians, and today we know of at least five major archaeological sites along the river system. Many more smaller sites are being discovered almost yearly. The valley not only can boast of containing the northern terminus of the Natchez Trace, which at one time probably was the most traveled overland road in the old Southwest, but also can claim as its own the childhood homes of such noted individuals as Matthew Fontaine Maury and Thomas Hart Benton.

Here then, in the pages that follow, is an attempt to make up for the years of neglect that a river, its valley, its places, and its people have suffered for lack of someone taking the time to make their history come alive through print.

Chapter 1

How the Harpeth Got Its Name — Maybe

No one knows who gave the name, Harpeth, to the lovely river that is the subject of this book, nor do we know how the word came into use to describe it. There have been several theories, but as far as can be determined, the true origin of the name is lost and probably will never be known.

Goodspeed's *History of Tennessee* indicates that the river was named after the Harpe Brothers. These two men, Micajah and Wiley, or as they have come down to us in history, Big Harpe and Little Harpe respectively, were outlaws who frequented this part of the country in the late 1790's and early 1800's. During that period, the Old Southwest as this section of the United States was then called, seemed to be plagued with a multitude of outlaws, thieves, murderers, and others of doubtful background. The Natchez Trace, which was about the only land route available at that time between Nashville and the lower Mississippi country, was a natural hunting ground for all of these various people since the Trace received quite a bit of foot and horse traffic at that time. During these early days it was customary for goods to be shipped down the Ohio to the Mississippi and thenceforth down to New Orleans for sale. The merchantmen not only sold their goods there, but would also sell their boats and other equipment. They would then set out on the Natchez Trace on foot or horseback to eventually wind up back on the Ohio, where they would take on another load of goods headed for New Orleans. Consequently, on the northbound, overland trip the travelers were usually fairly well endowed with money and thus provided easy pickings for those who preferred to steal what they could rather than work for it.

1. In the Valley of the Harpeth

This then was the setting for the entrance of the Harpe Brothers. These apparently psychotic killers were probably best remembered for the clever way in which they disposed of the body of a murder victim. They would slit the front of the body open, fill it with rocks, and then dump the entire package—body, rocks, and all—into the river to sink. Big Harpe can also be remembered for picking his own child up by the feet and smashing its brains out on a nearby tree. This was apparently done because the child's crying got on Micajah's nerves.

To get back to the origin of the name Harpeth, however, this theory does not stand up to careful examination. The Harpes do not appear in the Harpeth River-Natchez Trace area until the late 1790's, while there are records calling our river by the name Harpeth as early as 1784. Thus on the basis of this fact alone, it appears that this theory can be disregarded.

Another theory would place a more romantic aspect to the problem of the origin of the name Harpeth. This theory maintains that the river was named after a character appearing in *The Spectator,* an English classic of the eighteenth century. An issue of *The Spectator,* published in 1714, and a volume which could very well have been in the hands of the more educated members of the pioneer settlements, relates the story which forms the basis for this second theory. As the story goes, it seems that a certain young female descended from Cain fell in love with a young man by the name of Harpath. It appears that Harpath's brother also had eyes for this fair lady. Since Harpath had already won her love, the brother put a curse on him which would make it impossible for him to leave the river and valley lands which he then controlled. The curse must have instilled enough fear in Harpath that he didn't leave his homeplace for safety's sake. In one of his more careless moments, however, he fell into one of his own rivers and drowned. This river thereafter was forever known as the Harpath.

Whether or not our ancestors on the Harpeth were infatuated with this story to such an extent that they lifted the hero's name out of it to bestow on their familiar river may seem a little far-fetched. However, there are worse ways in which place names across the state and the country have evolved, so we can accept this theory as a possible explanation. Also lending credibility to this theory is that fact that several early maps show the river with the spelling H-A-R-P-A-T-H.

An intriguing aspect of this whole problem is the fact that both Haywood in at least two places in his book, *Civil and Political History of Tennessee,* and Breazeale in his book, *Life As It Is,* refer to our river as the Harper. In other places in their books they refer to it as the Harpeth. That both these gentlemen would refer to the same river by two different names seems a little strange. There can be no doubt that their Harper references are really referring to the Harpeth because of other place names in their text which pretty well isolate the locations to which they are referring. In one instance, Breazeale even refers to it as the Big Harper.

I wonder if the original name of the river could have been Harper and through the years been misconstrued into Harpeth. This could possibly account for the fact that both Haywood and Breazeale used the two names interchangeably. At the time when these men wrote their books, Haywood in 1823 and Breazeale in 1842, the original name could still have been in the memories of some people.

Of course, this theory has loopholes like all other theories. One serious argument against it is that apparently the word Harpeth in its present pronunciation was used to describe the river as early as 1784, which was just about as early as the pioneers seriously started settling the country thereabouts.

If the theory is true, we still have trouble. What is the origin of the name Harper? Since I have no idea what the answer to this last question is, and since it really doesn't have any bearing on our story, we will leave the problem with the above exploration of the three theories. About all else we can say is that we really don't know how the Harpeth River got its name.

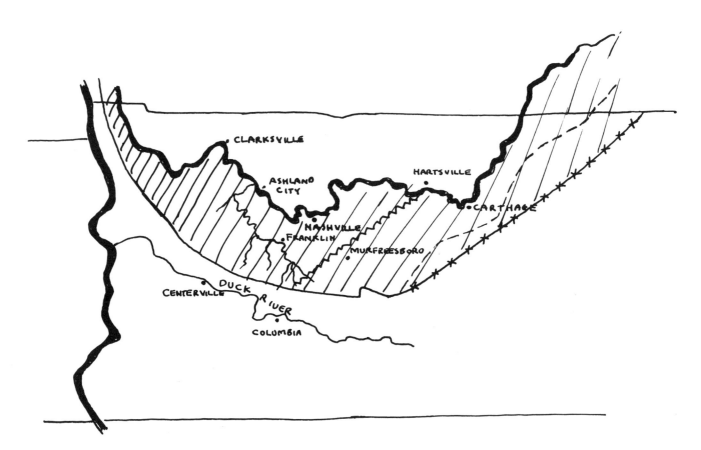

∧∧∧∧∧   TREATY LINE OF 1785 - LITERAL CONSTRUCTION.

- - - - -   TREATY LINE OF 1785 - WINCHESTER'S SURVEY.

✗ ✗ ✗   TREATY LINE OF 1785 - LATER CONSTRUCTION.

2. The Treaty of Hopewell

Chapter 2

The Treaty of Hopewell

The vast area of country lying between the Duck River on the south and the Cumberland River on the north and including all of the Harpeth River drainage area is part of a parcel of land ceded by the Cherokee Indians on November 18, 1785 within the terms of the Treaty of Hopewell. This treaty, the first one ever negotiated between representatives of the United States Government and the Cherokee Nation, was consummated in Hopewell, South Carolina.

The negotiations were handled on the part of the United States by four commissioners, namely Colonel Benjamin Hawkins of North Carolina, General Andrew Pickens of South Carolina, Cherokee Agent Joseph Martin of Tennessee (still part of North Carolina at that time), and Colonel Lachlan McIntosh of Georgia. Nine hundred and eighteen Cherokees attended the gathering, but only thirty-seven chiefs and principal men actually participated in the signing.

After explaining to the Cherokees that the governing power of the country had changed from Great Britain to the Congress of the United States since the outcome of the Revolution, the points of the treaty were discussed. There were thirteen points in all, and at the risk of burdening some of the readers with this much detail, all thirteen are given here, because I think they point out how one-sided this and all subsequent treaties were in favor of the whites.

Material Provisions

1. The Cherokees to restore to liberty all prisoners citizens of the United States or subjects of their allies; also, all negroes and other property taken from citizens during the late war.

2. The United States to restore to the Cherokees all Indian prisoners taken during the late war.

3. The Cherokees to acknowledge themselves under the exclusive protection of the United States.

4. The boundary line between the Cherokees' hunting-ground and the United States to be as follows, viz: Begin at the mouth of Duck River on the Tennessee; thence northeast to the ridge dividing the waters falling into Cumberland from those falling into the Tennessee; thence eastwardly along said ridge to a northeast line to be run, which shall strike Cumberland River 40 miles above Nashville; thence along said line to the river; thence up the river to the ford where the Kentucky road crosses; thence to Campbell's line near Cumberland Gap; thence to the mouth of Claud's Creek on Holstein; thence to Chimney-Top Mountain; thence to Camp Creek, near the mouth of Big Limestone on Nolichucky; thence southerly six (6) miles to a mountain; thence south to the North Carolina line; thence to the South top of Currohee Mountain; thence to the Carolina Indian boundary, and along the same southwest over the top of Oconee Mountain till it shall strike Tugaloo River; thence a direct line to the head of the fork of Oconee River.

5. Citizens of the United States or persons other than Indians who settle or attempt to settle on lands west or south of said boundary and refuse to remove within six months after ratification of this treaty to forfeit the protection of the United States, and the Indians to punish them or not, as they please: Provided, That this article shall not extend to the people settled between the fork of French Broad and Holstein Rivers, whose status shall be determined by Congress.

6. The Cherokees to deliver up for punishment all Indian criminals for offenses against citizens of the United States.

7. Citizens of the United States committing crimes against Indians to be punished by the United States in the presence of the Cherokees, to whom due notice of the time and place of such intended punishment shall be given.

8. Retaliation declared unjust and not to be practiced.

9. The United States to have sole right of regulating trade with the Indians and managing their affairs.

10. Traders to have liberty to trade with the Cherokees until Congress shall adopt regulations relative thereto.

11. Cherokees to give notice of any designs formed by other tribes against the peace, trade, or interests of the United States.

12. Cherokees to have the right to send a deputy of their choice to Congress whenever they think fit.

13. The hatchet to be forever buried between the United States and Cherokees.

Point Four, the real issue of this treaty, is extremely interesting in retrospect since the real boundary line defined by that section which reads "Thence eastwardly along said ridge to a northeast line to be run, which shall strike Cumberland River 40 miles above Nashville" was never really cleared up until twelve years later, and then probably incorrectly. The misunderstanding came about in determining whether the line was to strike the river 40 miles above Nashville or whether the line was to run to the river from the ridge 40 miles above Nashville. The former definition was apparently intended but due to a reiteration of the latter construction in a later treaty in 1791, this latter one was adopted. By 1797 when the boundary was actually surveyed, so many whites were living in the area between the two possible boundaries that the latter of necessity had to be adopted in order to maintain the legality of the earlier treaties.

The 918 Cherokees who attended this affair were awarded trade goods valued at about $1,300. It was explained that payment was this small because only the chiefs and headmen were expected at the signing. This little known example of the generosity of the white man toward the Indian, both in the amount of original payment and in the later acquisition of land not specifically related to in the treaty, rates fairly well with the classic case of Manhatten Island being bought from the Indians for $24.00.

Thus it became official that this vast fertile land forever more became the possession of the white man, not without additional bloodshed however. For the ridiculous price of $1,300, the Cherokees gave away some of the most beautiful, productive land in the state, indeed in the whole United States. No one can really be held responsible for this absurdity, I don't suppose. The whites were pushing for more and more space and this plot of land was the next logical space to be occupied. The Indians probably thought they were getting a good deal out of it. In later years this same story would be retold again and again when other Indians ceded other lands over to their white "brothers". And so it went, on and on, until eventually the entire State of Tennessee became the possession of the ever expanding white settlers.

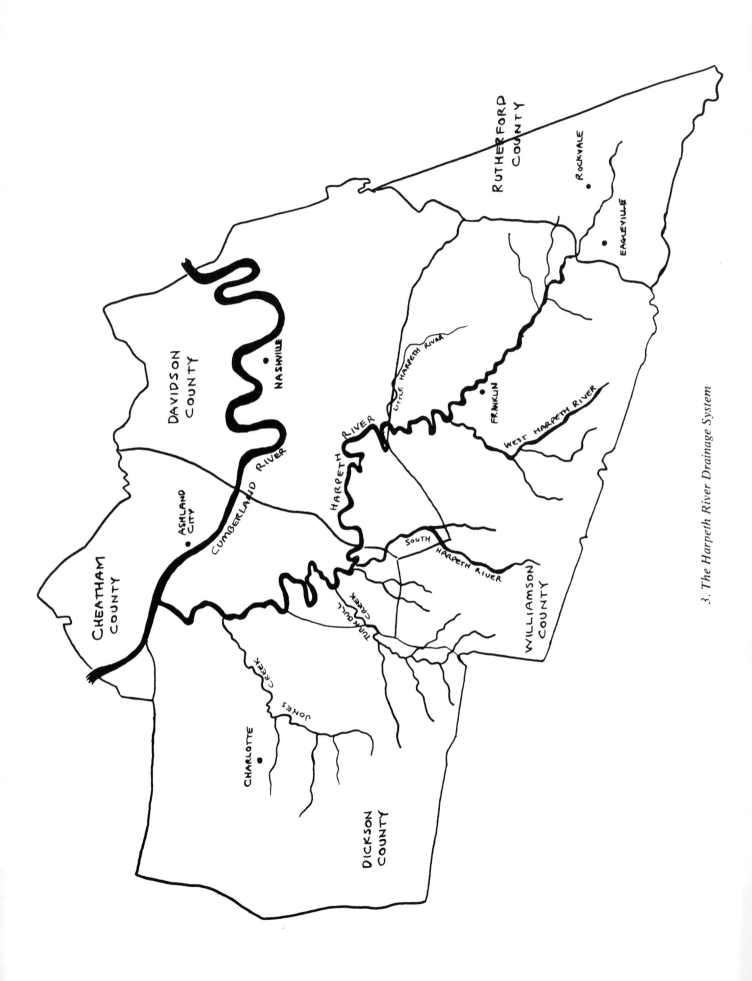

RUTHERFORD COUNTY

• ROCKVALE

• EAGLEVILLE

LITTLE HARPETH RIVER

• FRANKLIN

WEST HARPETH RIVER

HARPETH RIVER

SOUTH HARPETH RIVER

WILLIAMSON COUNTY

DAVIDSON COUNTY

• NASHVILLE

CUMBERLAND RIVER

ASHLAND CITY •

CHEATHAM COUNTY

TURNBULL CREEK

CREEK

JONES

CHARLOTTE •

DICKSON COUNTY

3. The Harpeth River Drainage System

Chapter 3

The Counties

Rutherford County has several distinctions among the areas surveyed in this book. First of all it is the county in which our story begins because in Rutherford County is the source of the Harpeth River. Rutherford also has less of the Harpeth flowing through it than any of the other four counties. Serving only the extreme southwestern portion of the county the Harpeth runs northwestward across the border into Williamson County. The rest of Rutherford's watershed area is drained by the Stones River, which has its source in the southeastern and eastern portions of the county and which drains into the Cumberland River at Donelson, upstream from Nashville.

Rutherford County also happens to be the largest of the Harpeth River counties with an area of 630 square miles. It lies at the exact geographical center of both middle Tennessee and the entire state as a whole. It has the highest population, 65,000, of the four rural counties in the area, being surpassed only by Davidson County.

Rutherford County was chartered in 1803 and formed of land that was originally part of Davidson County. General Griffith Rutherford of North Carolina, a Revolutionary War hero and a renowned Indian fighter in Tennessee as well, is credited with lending his name to the county.

Murfreesboro became the county seat of Rutherford County in 1811 and was founded on land originally owned by Captain William Lytle. Captain Lytle's memory lives on in the minds of the inhabitants of Murfreesboro through one of the downtown streets which was named in his honor. For a while Murfreesboro, originally spelled Murfreesborough, was the capital of the state. Murfreesboro received its name in honor of

Colonel Hardy Murfree of North Carolina. Colonel Murfree served in
the Revolutionary War and later moved to Tennessee, settling on Murfree's Branch of the West Harpeth River in Williamson County.

Rutherford County has a magnificent history all its own. However,
since the Harpeth River traverses only a small portion of this county, its
story will not be told in these pages outside of the brief sketch above.

Tradition has it that the first exploration of Williamson County was
done in 1797 when four men—Graham, Brown, Tindel, and an un-
identified Negro—and a dog were hunting bears in the vicinity of Holly
Tree Gap. This gap in the hills, sometimes known as Hollow Tree
Gap, has been the subject of quite a bit of argument as to its proper
location over the past few years. It is now generally believed to have
been on the present day Franklin Road at the pass through the hills just
before reaching Holly Tree Gap Road as one travels south.

These hunters located bear and shot one. The sound of the gunfire
apparently attracted some wandering Indians who set upon the four
men and killed them. Sometime after the skirmish, some other travelers
supposedly came upon the dog in a starved state, and he reportedly
led the travelers to the bodies of his dead masters.

Holly Tree Gap was crossed again in 1798 when four more travelers
passed through these parts. These four—George Neely, Andrew Goff,
William McEwen and David McEwen—are commemorated by a plaque
placed on the east side of Franklin Road at the top of the pass. This
same Holly Tree Gap was to become famous over the next few years
as a dangerous place to travel because of the vast number of robberies
and murders that occurred there.

Regardless of the original exploration of the area that was to become
Williamson County, an act by the General Assembly of Tennessee on
October 26, 1799 made the formation of the county a reality. It, like
Rutherford and part of Cheatham County, derived its land from David-
son County. Williamson County received its name in honor of Dr. Hugh
Williamson of North Carolina. Dr. Williamson was a Colonel in the
North Carolina Milita and also served as Surgeon-General for that body.
Dr. Williamson's stature in the national political picture of the times
is evidenced by the fact that he served for three terms in the Continental
Congress.

The county was settled largely by people with Revolutionary War
grants given to veterans for payment for their services to the country
during the War of Independence. On the same day that the act was

passed establishing Williamson County, it was also determined that the county seat should be Franklin, and the plan for this town was approved. The town, Franklin, received its name in honor of Benjamin Franklin, a very good friend of Dr. Hugh Williamson.

Before the county was formed a tract of land consisting of 3840 acres belonged to Anthony Sharp. On August 13, 1799 Sharp sold 640 acres of this land to Abram Maury for the price of $1,500. The future town of Franklin was to be formed on property that was part of this 640 acre purchase. Maury was a land speculator and he laid out lots in the newly organized town and sold them. The results of his speculation was the original town of Franklin consisting of 109 acres. The first house appeared in what was to become Franklin in 1797, some two years before the town was an official entity. On October 9, 1815 Franklin was incorporated.

Killebrew, in his classic *Resources of Tennessee,* published in 1874, had the following to say of Williamson County: "Much has been written about the famous blue grass lands of Kentucky, and the lands on the Mt. Pleasant Pike, near Columbia, are deservedly admired; but here is a whole county, as it were, equal to the best lands in any country." This land retains even to this day the beauty and value that Killebrew wrote of earlier. In 1964 there were 1772 farms in Williamson County consisting of 267,000 acres or 70.3 per cent of its 593 square miles. The average size of each farm was 125 acres each, with five farms consisting of over 1000 acres each. The value of farm products sold was over $9,000,000, which averages out to $4,045 per farm. The income from livestock exceeded that of crops by four and one-half to one. These acreage figures show the overwhelmingly rural nature of the county just as the income figures show the profitability of this rural endeavor.

Williamson County is the only one among the five counties in our discussion that can boast of having all four of the Harpeths flow within its confines. As a matter of fact three of the four have their sources in the county. All but the Harpeth River itself begin their journeys to the sea in various sections of Williamson County.

The Harpeth crosses the Williamson-Rutherford County line in the vicinity of Kirkland in the extreme south-east portion of the county. It does not leave Williamson again until it comes into Davidson County at the point where it meets with the Little Harpeth River on the boundary between Davidson and Williamson Counties.

The Little Harpeth never leaves the county for good since it dumps its waters into the Harpeth exactly on the Davidson-Williamson County line as referred to above. It does leave the county of its origin twice for brief journeys into Davidson County prior to its entry into the Big

Harpeth, but the Little Harpeth, except for these minor sojourns, is a total Williamson County river.

The West Harpeth has its beginnings in the south-central section of the county and it, like the Little Harpeth, never leaves the county for good. Unlike the Little Harpeth, however, it never even leaves the county at all. It then, even more than its little neighbor, is a total Williamson County river. The West Harpeth's mouth is close to the Del Rio Pike, where it flows into the Big Harpeth east of Forest Home.

The South Harpeth's source is in the western portion of the county between Craigfield and Leiper's Fork. Its entrance into Davidson County occurs near the Old Harding Road near Linton.

Williamson then can be called the real valley of the Harpeth since all four of the rivers flow for miles through this county. As we look at a map, we can easily see how this system of rivers is so important to Williamson above all other counties for the almost total drainage it provides for its land and its people.

The Harpeth River Basin consists of parts of five middle Tennessee counties: Williamson, Cheatham, Davidson, Dickson, and Rutherford. Of the five of these counties only Davidson was an official entity before Tennessee actually became a state. It was chartered by the State of North Carolina in 1783, just three years after the official settlement of Nashboro, later called Nashville, in 1780. It was named in honor of General William D. Davidson of North Carolina.

By comparing the two dates of the Treaty of Hopewell in 1785, and the chartering of Davidson County in 1783, it is apparent that a large part of Davidson County—which at that time was vastly larger than its present confines, and as will be seen, included much of the land used later in the formation of new middle Tennessee counties—was still officially Indian Territory when it became chartered by the State of North Carolina.

Of the four rivers bearing "Harpeth" in their name, only the West Harpeth does not flow at all in Davidson County. Even the three remaining streams—Harpeth, South Harpeth, and Little Harpeth—drain only a very small portion of Davidson County's 527 square miles. Only in the extreme southern and southwestern parts do these three streams meander across the face of present day Davidson County.

The Little Harpeth crosses the Davidson County border in the vicinity of the Edwin Warner Park picnic grounds off Vaughn's Road, only to flow for a few hundred feet and then go back into Williamson County. Here, in the county of its source it flows for about a half mile before turning northwestward again and going back into Davidson County. It follows its northwestward direction for about 2,000 feet or so, and then turns abruptly southward. After flowing southward for no more than three or four hundred feet, it then heads off in a southwestwardly direction back into Williamson County. A small meander and a turn northwestward again brings the Little Harpeth to its last look at Davidson County. Here, exactly at the Williamson-Davidson County line, is its mouth and its entrance into the Big Harpeth River. This converging of the waters of the largest and the smallest of the four Harpeth Rivers takes place just about a thousand feet upstream from the Highway 100 Bridge over the Big Harpeth in Davidson County.

The South Harpeth enters the county a little north of the Old Harding Road, south of Linton. It flows under the highway at Linton and goes off to the north alongside South Harpeth Road. It then forms the Cheatham-Davidson County border for about another mile before leaving Davidson County in the area where Davidson, Cheatham, and Williamson Counties come together.

The Big Harpeth comes into the county from the southwest, flowing northeastwardly alongside Highway 100 for about a half mile, going back into Williamson County for just a few hundred feet and then back into Davidson at the point where the Little Harpeth converges with it. It then turns north and flows under Highway 100. For the next few miles the Harpeth meanders lazily through the county, under the Old Harding Road southwest of Bellevue, alongside U. S. Highway 70 for a while, past Newsom's Mill, and finally leaves Davidson and enters Cheatham County about a mile and a half southeast of Pegram.

Cheatham County is affected by two of the Harpeths: The South Harpeth and the Harpeth itself. Cheatham is not only the smallest county in the Harpeth Valley with 305 square miles, but it is also the least populated with only 12,400 people. A little over one half of the land is used for farming purposes according to 1964 figures. At that time some 99,000 acres were defined as farm property. The average size farm in Cheatham County was 114 acres, with the value of farm products sold averaging $2,717 per farm in 1964.

Cheatham County was formed by an act of the Tennessee General Assembly on February 28, 1856. It was created from portions of Davidson, Robertson, Montgomery, and Dickson Counties. Cheatham is fairly well evenly divided into northern and southern portions by the Cumberland River. The entire area to the north is drained by the Cumberland and its tributary system while the majority of that to the south drains into the Harpeth. There are a few exceptions where some southern streams flow directly into the Cumberland. Ashland City, the county seat, is in the northern portion and thus out of the scope of the book. As a matter of interest however, it was surveyed and laid out as a town in 1856.

Kingston Springs is situated in the southern portion of the county and is the largest community in that section. It at one time was noted for its red, white, and black sulphur water according to Killebrew in his *Resources of Tennessee,* published in 1874. It is situated in a bend of the Big Harpeth River on the old Nashville, Chattanooga, and St. Louis railway line.

Cheatham contains two of our rivers named Harpeth: the Harpeth itself and the South Harpeth. The South Harpeth enters Cheatham at the extreme southeast corner of the county and flows about four miles in a northwestwardly direction before entering the Harpeth about two miles southwest of Pegram. The Big Harpeth also enters the county in the southeast and meanders for several miles toward the northwest, creating a magnificent set of river bends in doing so. The river finally reaches the Dickson-Cheatham County border and flows generally northward, serving as the border between these two counties until it reaches the Cumberland River at Harpeth Shoals, below Ashland City.

Perhaps more so than the other counties surveyed in this book, Cheatham has maintained its primitive beginnings. Much of the land is still clothed in forest and is a haven for wildlife. Cheatham County boasts a fine state supported wildlife management area and a beautiful lake on the Cumberland, named after this county through which it flows.

The first white man is said to have been present in what is now Dickson County as early as 1786. The area was explored in depth later, with the majority of its original settlers obtaining their land from military land grants given to Revolutionary War Veterans. The county was officially created on October 25, 1803, the land utilized for its formation coming from holdings previously in Robertson and Montgomery Counties. These two parent counties were already entities, having been created under the authority of the Territory of the United States of America, South of the Ohio River. The new county received its name in honor of a Nashville physician, William Dickson.

Dickson County did not hold on to its new dimensions for long, because just four years later on December 3, 1807, the total area was reduced when part of Dickson was acquired for the formation of Hickman County. On October 19, 1809, almost six years to the day from its formation, it again had to relinquish more land—this time to the formation of Humphreys County. This new size persisted for some years, but again on February 22, 1856, more land was taken from Dickson for its new neighbor, Cheatham County. Finally, on January 23, 1871, the last parcel of land was acquired from Dickson for the formation of a new county, this time Houston. Since this last time, the county has maintained a constant size. For over one hundred years it has contained its present 485 square miles.

The county seat of Charlotte was laid out in 1804 on land originally owned by Charles Stewart. A commission had been set up to select a county seat, and Stewart donated the property which lay on Town Branch—a tributary of Jones Creek, which in turn is a tributary to the Big Harpeth River—for this purpose.

Only the Harpeth, of the four rivers named Harpeth, affects Dickson County. For some eleven miles or so as the crow flies, and for several more than that as the river flows, the Harpeth River moves along in a generally northward direction to form a common boundary between Cheatham and Dickson Counties. Beaverdam Creek and Nails Creek, both entirely in Dickson County, dump their waters into Turnbull Creek which flows through Dickson County, but which has its source in Williamson County and its mouth in Cheatham. Jones Creek, further on downstream from the mouth of the Turnbull, is the carrier of water from several smaller streams, and it releases its load of water directly into the Harpeth about midway of that stretch of the big river which serves as the boundary line between the two counties.

The Harpeth itself picks up waters from other, smaller streams in its meandering journey between Dickson and Cheatham Counties. Finally though it reaches its destination at the Cumberland River and here, a few miles downstream from Ashland City in the back reaches of Cheatham Lake, it dumps its load collected from the hundreds of tributaries all the way back to Rutherford County.

4. Old-Fashioned Gas Pump on Wilson Pike

Chapter 4

The
Little Harpeth
River

The Little Harpeth River has the distinction of being the only one of the three Harpeth-named tributaries to the Big Harpeth to flow into it on its right bank. Both the South and West Harpeths approach from the left. The Little Harpeth is the second of these three to flow into the big Harpeth, the number one honor being reserved for the West Harpeth.

The Little Harpeth starts its approximate fourteen mile journey to its rendevous with the Harpeth down alongside Wilson Pike in the north-east portion of Williamson County. It flows from there in a generally northerly direction for a while, then turns northwestward and ends up flowing almost due west just before it enters the Harpeth on the Davidson-Williamson County line.

This stream, the shortest of the four Harpeths, flows through some of the most beautiful land in the county. Killebrew, in his *Resources of Tennessee,* commented upon the fine lands and their values in the following passage: "The lands on this stream are as rich as the richest, and generally are finely improved, and are graced with the best country residences in the county. Land is here in great demand, as high as $100 per acre being occasionally paid, and $75 to $80 per acre being quite common." The reference to the price that land brought in this area is almost unbelievable when considering the value of the same land today. But, when we remember that this book was written almost one hundred years ago, I suppose that the price of $100 per acre for a commodity as common as land did seem extremely high in view of the fact that it was selling in other places for just a few dollars an acre and less.

The exact source of the Little Harpeth is a spring on the grounds of "Inglehame", presently owned by Mr. and Mrs. Vernon Sharp. The intermittent stream which issues forth from the spring, plus several other streams of like nature, finally come together to form what can really be called the Little Harpeth River, even though at the time, it is still hardly more than a small creek.

"Inglehame" was built in 1855 by Colonel James Hazard Wilson, Sr. Colonel Wilson was a man of great wealth, owning property in several southern states at the time. The original name of this beautiful home and farm was "Harpeth". Colonel Wilson is also responsible for the construction of "Ravenwood", which lies across the road from "Inglehame". "Ravenwood" was built several years earlier than "Harpeth", and is now owned by Mr. and Mrs. Reese Smith.

The Wilson Pike, which of course was named in honor of Colonel Wilson, separates these two great farms. This pike, which was originally a toll road, connects Brentwood on the north with Arrington on the south. At one time, according to an 1878 map in the State Library in Nashville, its name used to be Harpeth Pike.

The Little Harpeth River flows under the Wilson Pike just after its beginnings and flows alongside it for several miles before veering off to the northwest. The river and the pike are accompanied along this part of the journey by the Louisville and Nashville Railroad. The tracks, part of the eastern branch from Athens, Alabama, go through Lewisburg and meet with the western branch from Athens just south of Brentwood. The railroad and Wilson Pike play leap frog all the way from Arrington to Brentwood, each changing sides with the other four times during the thirteen mile journey.

About a mile and a half from its source the Little Harpeth flows under Moore's Lane. Lying just to the south of the road can still be seen one of the large mounds that was part of the huge Indian village that eons ago lay on this place. This area, known as the Fewkes Site, was excavated several years ago under the auspices of the Bureau of American Ethnology of the Smithsonian Institution, and many artifacts were found which have greatly increased our knowledge of prehistoric man in this area. Further information regarding the Fewkes Site will be reserved until we reach chapter 12, which is totally dedicated to this prehistoric village.

In the same location, however, is another site of historical interest. As one looks at the large mound in the Fewkes Site just off Moore's Lane, he cannot help but wonder about the two storied red brick building that sets just off to the side of the mound. This quaint little building is Boiling Springs Academy. It apparently derived its name from the

5. Boiling Springs Academy

springs which issue forth on the property and provide sustenance for the Little Harpeth. Boiling Springs Academy was established as a learning institution, within the Academy System, in 1830. The Academy System was provided for by the State of Tennessee in order to fulfill the educational void that was present at that time. The law providing for the establishment of the public high school system was not passed until 1899. Before this time then the academies were about the only place that provided an education for the general public.

There were several reasons for the establishment of the Academy System. One such reason was a response to the "New Democracy" that became evident in the early years of the nineteenth century. After Thomas Jefferson became President of the United States in 1801, academies sprang up in states all over the then existing country. It was felt that children well educated in Greek, Latin, history, and other such subjects offered by most academies would provide the country with the responsible, aware citizenry that this "New Democracy" called for.

A more practical reason was provided by the desire for an educational system that would fully prepare its students for college. The Tennessee Legislature in its "Act of 1817" made this point clear when it stated, "Be it enacted that all the academies of this state shall be considered schools preparatory to the introduction of students into college."

Prior to 1860 the Academy System in Tennessee was supported by the proceeds derived from the sale of land that had already been reserved and set aside by the State and/or National Governments for these purposes. As needed these lands were sold specifically in order to provide funds for the system. In addition to this, tuition was charged for attendance, the fees varying upon which academy was attended.

Boiling Springs was the second such academy established in Williamson County, the first being established in 1829, only one year prior to Boiling Springs. Academies in general were divided into four types with respect to who could attend: Male Only, Female Only, Male and Female, and Unclassified. Boiling Springs, according to the records, was Unclassified, meaning, I suppose, that anyone could attend. The Boiling Springs Academy buildling was in later years, after it ceased to be a learning institution, converted into a Presbyterian Church and apparently served in that capacity until its final desertion.

Both the Fewkes Site and Boiling Springs Academy lie on the T. P. Primm, Sr. property and I have discussed both places with Miss Ruby Primm, who teaches in the Nashville-Metro School System. Miss Primm's family has lived on this property from the earliest settlement of this part of the country. Their property was acquired through land grant from the government and the original home was built in 1806. Part of the original log house is still visible in the old homeplace on Moore's Lane. Miss Primm's grandmother was a Thompson and the family owned property in Davidson County also. Some of this land contains the present day Thompson Lane in Nashville, named in the family's honor.

Moore's Lane runs into Wilson Pike just a short distance to the east of the Boiling Springs Academy building. This junction in the last century was a little more active than it is now. A cotton gin used to set in the mouth of Moore's Lane on the east side of Wilson Pike between the pike and the railroad. A small store shared the corner also. Driving through this rural country today, it is difficult to visualize much more activity ever happening than that which is going on now. The cotton gin was one of several in Williamson County and it is interesting to note that this crop, which is practically nonexistent in the area now, must have been one of the more common products one hundred years ago.

A short distance north on the Wilson Pike from Moore's Lane, lies "Forge Seat". This beautiful home was built in 1808 by Samuel and Andrew Crockett, who ran a forge in the area. Tradition has it that another Crockett—David, no relation—passed this way and paid a visit to "Forge Seat" as he made his way to battle the Mexicans at the Alamo.

This reference to David Crockett and the Mexican conflict is ironic in that the Wilson Pike crosses the Williamson County line from Davidson and, upon its entry into Williamson, runs south through the 15th Civil District of the county for quite a distance. It was the 15th District of Williamson which had the unique distinction of having every male between the ages of 18 and 35 to volunteer their services for the United States Army during the Mexican War. This response to duty for country was so overwhelming and unanimous that lots had to be drawn among the volunteers to determine who was to remain on the home front with the women, children, and the elderly. With enthusiasm such as this, it is no wonder that Tennessee retained its nickname, Volunteer State, which it had earned during the War of 1812.

The Wilson Pike's first toll gate was on the southwest corner of Old Smyrna Road and Wilson Pike. To the west of Wilson Pike Old Smyrna Road ran past the new Brentwood Railroad Station, which is now gone. Old Smyrna terminates its western arm at the Franklin Road, across from the country club. This arm of the road has been bisected by the interstate highway, but it picks up on the west side of I-65 where it left off on the east. On the east side of Wilson Pike, Old Smyrna goes off to meet with the Edmondson Pike in Davidson County, and in so doing

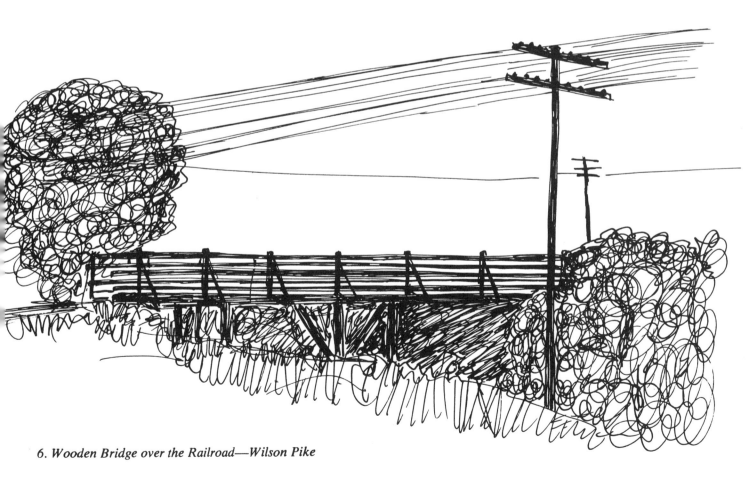

6. Wooden Bridge over the Railroad—Wilson Pike

7. Old House on Smyrna Road

crosses two of the small intermittent streams that are tributary to the Little Harpeth.

By this time the Little Harpeth River has angled out into more of a northwestwardly direction and has flowed under the western fork of the Louisville and Nashville Railroad. This fork, which leaves its eastern branch at Athens, Alabama, runs through Columbia, Thompson's Station, and Franklin before rejoining it in the vicinity of the Old Smyrna Road.

The Little Harpeth continues on its way until it approaches the Franklin Road, U. S. Highway 31. Here it flows under the highway and into the Brentwood Country Club grounds. Franklin Road was originally known as the Franklin Turnpike. Brentwood served as the northern terminus and Franklin served as the southern terminus. An extension of this road with Franklin at the north and Spring Hill at the south was known as the Franklin and Spring Hill Turnpike. The Franklin Turnpike was chartered for construction in November of 1830, with the road being completed in 1834. Later this road was called the Andrew Jackson Highway, and more recently the Franklin Pike or Road.

The Brentwood Country Club occupies the grounds and residence originally known as "Midway", because it lay halfway between Nashville and Franklin. "Midway" was built in 1829 by Lysander McGavock. Partially destroyed by fire seventeen years later, the home was rebuilt, and it is this residence that can be seen today. "Midway" farm at one time reached on the north as far as Old Hickory Boulevard, and contained what is now known as Meadowlake and Iroquois Sub-Divisions. From this large estate came the clay that was used for the bricks that were utilized in the construction of "Midway".

An Indian mound was supposedly on the grounds at "Midway", and judging from recent discoveries in this area, there was probably a large concentration of prehistoric people in these parts. We have already made note of the Fewkes Site which, as the crow flies, lies only about five or six miles away. Now, here on the original "Midway" property and what was later to become the A. J. Dyer farm, we come across evidence of another Indian habitation, although not as large as that at Fewkes.

On a tiny intermittent stream that flows into the Little Harpeth River from the north, and lying generally southeast of the Dyer residence between it and Midway House, lies what was known as the Arnold Site. Named after popular singer Eddie Arnold who was developer of the property at the time of discovery, this site was excavated in 1965 as rapidly as possible in order not to hamper the construction of the new homes in the area.

The excavated area was largely composed of the stone-lined graves which are so common in this area and which have become known as a hallmark of prehistory in the Middle Tennessee area.

While to my knowledge no mounds were present upon the property excavated, and the digging was confined to simple grave opening, there was apparently at one time a sizable mound just to the south of the residence and on the east side of the lake. A man told me while excavation was going on in 1965 that several years ago he could remember seeing the ends of the grave stones protruding from the ground where erosion had washed the top soil away. This mound was barely distinguishable as a slight rise in 1965, and now a residence sets on its approximate location.

Some charcoal was discovered at the site in the roadbed that was soon to become clustered by houses. Later in the season some fire pits, which when active indicate the center of the living dwelling, were discovered and also a few post molds. The presence of these remains would indicate that a habitation site existed here in addition to the burial grounds, but certainly it did not reach the proportions of the classic sites of Old Town, Fewkes, and some others in the Harpeth River valley.

The bodies in the excavated graves were placed there in the fully stretched-out position as opposed to the flexed-knee position common in some graves. A grave containing three bodies was opened at this site. This was a rare find in that it appeared that two adults and a child occupied the grave. Possibly this could have been a family group, and if this is true we can hardly help but wonder what common disaster brought death to all three at one time.

While some of the other sites described in this book are still visible, some more than others mainly because they happen to be in a more rural country, the Arnold Site is a thing of the past. The front yard of a residence occupies the spot where the main dig took place at this site and where the triple burial described above was found. The quiet stream above whose shallow banks this site was located is now reduced to no more than a drain through yards and through culverts under roads. Little children and dogs play now where several hundred years ago another tribe of little children and dogs played on the same ground, around the same stream, and under the same sky.

8. Old Barn on the Little Harpeth

Flowing ever onward, picking up more strength as it goes along, the Little Harpeth flows under the Granny White Pike about a mile south of Old Hickory Boulevard. Granny White Pike in the old days was sometimes called the Middle Franklin Pike because it lay between the Franklin Turnpike and the Hillsboro Pike both of which went to Franklin. It used to be a stage coach route south of Nashville linking up with other roads and exiting onto the Franklin Pike in the vicinity of the present day Holly Tree Gap Road.

Continuing on its northwestward journey the Little Harpeth runs under the Johnson Chapel Road and through some beautiful country until it reaches Hillsboro Road. The Little Harpeth forms the back border of a couple of sub-divisions through here, and with the ever expanding population of Metropolitan Nashville-Davidson County continuing to grow, this beautiful area along the Davidson-Williamson County border will probably continue to become crowded with suburban dwellings.

As the Little Harpeth flows under the Hillsboro Road, it generally straightens its direction out to flow more or less westward until it reaches its destination with the Big Harpeth. Just to the north of the river as it passes under the Hillsboro Road is located Harpeth Presbyterian Church.

The present building of this church was begun in 1836 on a portion of land donated by the McCutchen family from land received by the elder McCutchen for services rendered in the Revolutionary War. The church was organized twenty-five years prior to that, however, and was housed in a small log building until the present structure was begun.

During the years of construction of the present building the minister of Harpeth Presbyterian was Oliver Bliss Hayes. Hayes was the father of Adelicia Hayes who married Joseph Acklen. The Acklen's homeplace, "Belmont", was one of the most famous and beautiful homes in Nashville and the entire South. A son of Hayes, Henry, also resided in Nashville at "Ensworth". This estate consisted of what we know today as the West End section of Nashville. The homeplace stood on Hayes Street and is now a part of St. Thomas Hospital. Another son, O. B. Hayes, Jr., married Emily McGavock who was the daughter of Lysander McGavock, buildler of "Midway". This couple resided on the Midway Farm in their home called "Hayesland".

About a half mile downstream from the Harpeth Presbyterian Church the Little Harpeth receives water from two of its largest tributaries— Otter Creek, flowing in from the northeast and draining a sizable area in southern Davidson County between the Hillsboro and Franklin Roads, and Beech Creek, coming in from the southeast and draining the area from Hillsboro Road alongside Beech Creek Road back to Murray Lane on the west side of Granny White Pike.

About four miles upstream on Otter Creek from where it enters the Little Harpeth, lies Radnor Lake. This lake, which was built by damming Otter Creek, gathers its water from springs and ground water among some of the highest hills in Davidson County. Otter Creek falls about 185 feet in its four mile run from the lake to its mouth.

Radnor Lake was the brainchild of John Howe Peyton who was at the time Locating Engineer for the Lewisburg and Northern Railroad. He later became President of the Nashville, Chattanooga, and St. Louis Railroad. It was the purpose of Mr. Peyton's lake to furnish the entire water supply for Radnor Yards, the Louisville and Nashville Railroad's make-up and switching yard south of Nashville. The lake was completed in 1914, but was not used by the railroad until 1919.

The dam holding back the waters of the lake has a concrete core and the spillway elevation is 775 feet above sea level. The lake is situated on property bought by the railroad from several owners in the area, the majority of the original 900 acres coming from the Lea Estate. The lake surface itself contains about 85 acres, and a maximum depth of 45 feet is reached. During its normal stage, Radnor Lake contains 450,000,000 gallons of water.

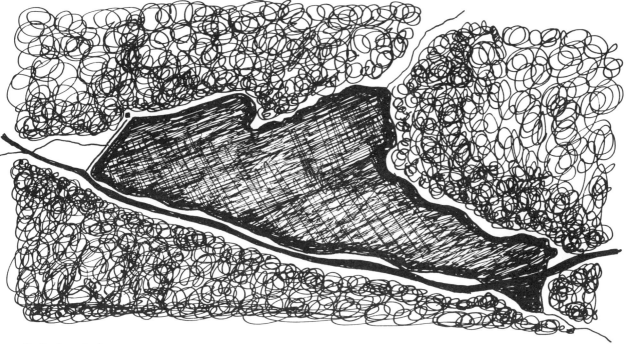

9. Radnor Lake

The Little Harpeth River flows under Vaughn Road near Edwin
Warner Park picnic grounds. Here was the first crossing of any river
called Harpeth for the Natchez Trace Road, which was built by the
United States Army in 1801-02. The road followed pretty generally
present day Vaughn Road from the vicinity of Old Hickory Boulevard
all the way to Sneed Road and beyond.

A few hundred feet beyond Vaughn Road the Little Harpeth makes
its first debut into Davidson County and its first exit from Williamson
County. For just one small meander does it linger in this alien county
before flowing for about a half mile more in Williamson. It then turns
again into Davidson for one last look before flowing back into Williamson for the second time.

The end is near now. Just a few more feet of flow in Williamson and
the Little Harpeth finally divests itself of its load into the Big Harpeth
River on the county line just at the northern turn of Hicks Bend in the
Harpeth. Thus for fourteen miles has the Little Harpeth flowed, from its
beginning as a spring and an unimportant intermittent creek to its ending as a respectable sized stream, truly worthy of the name river. For
fourteen miles and eons of time, the Little Harpeth has flowed through

the history of our land—from its earliest beginnings at Fewkes and Arnold Sites, through early pioneer times at Harpeth Presbyterian and Boiling Springs, right on down to the present at Edwin Warner Picnic Grounds and sub-divisions with such fanciful names as Wildwood Valley and River Oaks.

Chapter 5

The South Harpeth River

Within an area of Williamson County roughly forming a triangle—with Pinewood Road, Highway 100, and Highway 96 composing the three sides—lies the headwaters of the South Harpeth River. The three corners of this triangle are the communities of Leiper's Fork, Craigfield, and Fairview. Here within less than a two mile span the waters of Arkansas, South Harpeth, and Caney Fork Creeks all come together to form the South Harpeth River just south of the Fernvale community.

The South Harpeth is the western-most of the three Harpeth-named tributaries to the Big Harpeth, and it is the western part of Williamson County that this stream drains, along with a small portion of extreme southwestern Davidson County and southeastern Cheatham County. The South Harpeth flows almost due north for most of its length, turning slightly eastward to enter Davidson County and slightly westward to leave it.

This river runs through more "primitive" country than its sister streams. Primitive in this usage has no bearing on the cultural achievements of the inhabitants. The word is used to express the more wilderness aspects of some of the country that the South Harpeth flows through. There is much timber still in its watershed area, as compared to farmlands. This has always been true. While Killebrew, in his *Resources of Tennessee,* was extolling the valley of the Little Harpeth for its fine country residences and the high value of the land there, he was telling of the abundance of wild game and timber still to be found at that time on the South Harpeth. He said that the entire region was very sparsely settled and that the main economy of the area was its timber. He was overpowered by the fine stands of white oak, poplar, and chest-

nut along with the numbers of deer, turkey, and bear found in these
forests. Killebrew even went so far as to express his belief that this area
of Williamson County could provide much of the timber needs for the
entire Mississippi Valley. Comparing the land values between the two
areas he stated, "Lands sell here for from twenty-five cents to two
dollars per acre." Today, while the virgin growths of the fine timber
stands referred to in Killebrew are gone, the country along the South
Harpeth River is more of a forest nature than other sections of Williamson County.

One reason for the more primitive nature of this river is the rough
country it flows through. All of the more important source streams of
the South Harpeth have their beginnings in highland regions averaging
800-900 feet above sea level. The mouth of the river in Cheatham
County, where it dumps its waters into the Harpeth River, lies at the 500
foot level. Thus the river drops some 300-400 feet in its fairly short
journey.

10. A Deserted Church Beyond Fernvale

Among the many features of interest in this valley was one which appeared on the South Harpeth River and which has long since been gone. This was the famous summer resort hotel which used to stand near the present community of Fernvale on the Old Harding Road. Originally called Smith's Springs, after the original owner, the hotel and its associated springs drew visitors from all over the southeastern United States to sample the medicinal waters which allegedly cured just about every kind of ailment a person could possibly have.

The huge hotel that eventually stood at Smith's Springs and the one that followed it after the original one burned derived the majority of their customers from the Gulf Coast States. When these hotels were popular, in the late 1800's and very early 1900's, there were portions of our country, particularly the deep South, which were still subjugated in the summer time to yellow fever. The inhabitants of these fever-stricken areas, with their desire to escape the hot, moist, summer-time climate of their homes, kept the resort hotel business thriving. Hotels of this nature sprang up all over this part of the country, and their decline in the first couple of decades of the twentieth century was probably directly related to a combination of factors, among them the increasing control of yellow fever and its vector, the mosquito, the decreasing dependence that people had on mineral waters and its effect upon the human body, and the increasing popularity of other vacation lands, such as Florida.

In any event, during this period resort hotels held tremendous popularity. Some are still around such as Red Boiling Springs and Beersheba Springs in Tennessee and on a much larger scale, White Sulphur Springs in West Virginia. Evidence for Smith's Springs popularity can be found by referring once again to Killebrew:

> "It is on this stream that are situated the celebrated medicinal springs, well known as Smith's Springs. It is a very cool, pleasantly tasted water, and is moderately impregnated with iron, and strongly with sulphur, and has a great local reputation for curing diseases of the liver, kidneys, and bowels. This place only lacks a convenient method of travelling to make it popular, and is destined, when it is properly improved, to become one of our standard places of summer resort."

The Smiths, after whom Smith's Springs received its name, was one of the oldest families along the South Harpeth River. Their land was apparently granted to them for government services. A descendant of another old Williamson County family, John B. McEwen, bought the Smith property including the springs. While attempting to think of a different name for the springs, McEwen's wife's niece suggested that the area be called Fernvale Springs, because of the abundance of lush fern

11. Mayfield Springs

plants that could be found all over the hills and hollows. Thus it was
that the springs received their present name.

The original hotel structure upon this site burned in the waning days
of the 19th century. This was the hotel to which the visitors from the
Gulf Coast flocked in the summer time to take advantage of both the
cool pleasant climate and the healing mineral waters from the springs.
After the fire, the hotel was rebuilt and re-opened in June of 1901, with
Robert McEwen as manager. This new wooden structure boasted 114
rooms, a new ice house capable of storing 125 tons of ice, and garden
fresh vegetables at meal time. The big white hotel sat astride the Harding
Road, with a breezeway connecting the buildings on either side of the
road. An advertisement of the day gave the following prices:

Meals	$.50
Board and Lodging	1.00 per day
	7.00 per week
	29.00 per month

All this is quite a change from today when you have to pay $28.00 per
day for a decent hotel room, without meals! How times have changed!
The advertisement goes on to boast that as a health resort:

"Fernvale needs no advertisement. For all diseases of the stomach, kidney, bowels, skin, and eyes, these Springs have no superior, if an equal. For dyspepsia and kidney troubles they are almost a specific. For teething children in their second summer, it is a paradise. For nervous and physical exhaustion, from whatever causes, a few weeks sojourn and rest in this place will work wonders."

It can thus be seen from the above benefits that Fernvale drew as much of its popularity from those seeking cures to various and sundry ailments as it did from those folks escaping the mosquito-ridden Gulf Coast.

For those visitors coming from places such as Alabama, the Springs were accessible by train from Montgomery via Franklin. Nashville visitors could reach Fernvale by train also, either by going through Franklin or by going through Bellevue on the NC&StL line. Guests from Memphis could also ride the NC&StL line to Bellevue. Of course Franklin and Bellevue being as close as the train came, the rest of the journey was made by carriage or horseback.

For amusement while guests at the hotel, the visitors could participate in such pastimes as hunting, trout fishing, hiking, or ten pins. In the Ball Room, the music for dancing was provided by Professor De Pierrei of Nashville and his orchestra. Liquor was available from Franklin, but no gambling was permitted on the premises.

Around 1905 the hotel, springs, and some 3300 acres of surrounding

12. Sign Commemorating Fernvale Springs

land changed hands again. Mr. Bruce, father of Mr. Pepper Bruce, Sr. who still lives on adjoining property, bought the site in 1905 and continued to operate the springs for about two more years. Its popularity began to wane about this time, however, and business was not what it used to be. Then in about March of 1906 the huge wooden hotel caught fire and was completely destroyed.

All evidence of the two hotels which once provided rest and recreation for hundreds of people are gone. The springs are still there, however; one of them, the Mayfield Spring, can be seen from the road. It is rather difficult to stand in front of the white lattice work that covers this spring and try to imagine the hubbub of activity that once took place here and in the surrounding area not too many years ago. The sign erected in front of the spring house, I guess, best expresses the mood of the place:

> "Those of you who were here
> Now are old and very few
> Should you return for a bit of cheer
> We surely welcome you."

Another place of interest in the South Harpeth Valley is Caney Fork Furnace. Lying on the banks of the creek of the same name, the only remaining evidence of this place is to the right of the road as one leaves Fernvale. Hidden among the vines and bushes about fifty feet off the road are the remains of part of the furnace, consisting of many huge limestone blocks which once made up the main section of the complex. If one lets his imagination run wild with him a moment it is almost like looking at part of a lost city in the jungle. Standing at least twenty feet above the surrounding land and still in neat formation, these stones remind me of pictures I have seen of Machu Piccu high in the Andes when the fabled Inca City was first "discovered" in 1911 by Hiram Bingham.

But we don't have to go to South America for adventure. We have it right here in the ruins of the Old Caney Fork Furnace in the South Harpeth River Valley. This section of Williamson County is on the eastern edge of a rich iron-bearing stretch of country which includes Dickson, Lewis, Hickman and some other Middle Tennessee counties. We'll read shortly in the chapter on the Harpeth River of the exploits of Montgomery Bell, an early Tennessee ironmaster who maintained several forges in the Harpeth River Valley. Apparently Bell had nothing to do with this furnace and forge on Caney Fork Creek. It was probably operational about the same time as Bell's furnaces were however.

We don't know to what extent this furnace supplied the iron needs

13. Caney Fork Furnace

for the growing population in this part of the country. Probably it was sufficient for the majority of the needs. Of course Bell's furnaces probably gave quite a bit of healthy competition. We do know of one "sale" that the Caney Fork Furnace made however. The outside pillars in the Williamson County Courthouse in Franklin were cast at this furnace. The Courthouse was built in 1858 so the furnace must have been in operation over some considerable period of time.

If we let our imagination wander a little bit we can visualize the activity that took place at the forge in the late 1850's in preparation for this large order. Perhaps in addition to the order for the pillars, the forge was busy turning out cannon and other war material which would later be used in the Civil War. Surely it was obvious by 1858 that it could not be too much longer before the rift separating Northern and Southern philosophies would grow so wide that it would be incapable of being mended. There must have been talk among the workmen of the mounting differences between the two factions that were growing more and more obvious with every passing day.

In any event if we could go back in time to this period we would see the dense smoke arising from the furnaces and dissapating gradually into the air. Remember this furnace was located pretty deeply in the country, far away from civilization outside of a farm here and there. To come across such an establishment here in the wilderness would indeed give quite a startle. Nestled in the little valley of Caney Fork Creek, the furnace and its associated industry relied on the swift moving waters of this creek to furnish the water power necessary for the running of a forge.

14. Williamson County Courthouse

When the big day came and the pillars were complete, there must have been quite a bit of activity around the place. The ox-carts were made ready for the difficult trip ahead. It would have been necessary to start the journey early in the morning in order not to have spent the night on the road. It was quite a job lifting the pillars onto the carts, but at last with the assistance of many men and a handy block and tackle the task was finally completed.

We don't know what route from Caney Fork Furnace that the ox-carts took in transporting their cargo to Franklin. Perhaps from the forge they descended the trail beside the creek until they reached what is now Fernvale. From here they could have followed Old Harding Road, past Smith's Springs, until they came to the intersection with Old Charlotte Road. Old Charlotte Road would have taken them into Franklin. Admittedly, this last phase of the journey would have been pretty

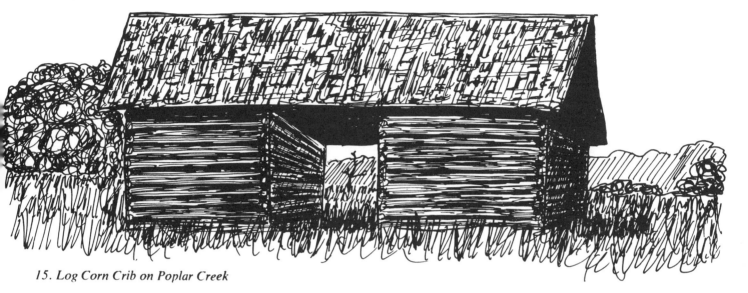

15. Log Corn Crib on Poplar Creek

difficult as anyone who has ever travelled over Old Charlotte Road with its hills and dells could testify. However, I suspect any route taken for a journey this long by ox-cart pulling several tons weight would be a difficult one.

At last Franklin was in sight and in a few more minutes the precious cargo was deposited in the town square. In a few more weeks the iron pillars were erected. And thus a small iron forge on the banks of a little Williamson County stream, a forge very few people today realize ever existed, added its part to the growing town of Franklin.

By the time the South Harpeth reaches the Davidson County line it is a considerable sized stream. Between the county line and Highway 100 the river goes under the old iron bridge* which has recently been replaced by a new structure on New Highway 96. The river then flows by several church camps and finally flows under the highway at Linton. Continuing northward it receives the waters of Poplar Creek from the east on the Davidson-Cheatham County line. Continuing a little further the South Harpeth at last releases its clear waters into the Big Harpeth near Buffalo Gap.

And so, this western most of the Harpeths reaches its end in Cheatham County. Described by Killebrew as being a little different than the other three Harpeths in its physical make-up, it weaves its way through three counties before arriving at its destination, and in so doing it weaves its tales across the years.

* This bridge has been destroyed since this book was written.

16. Cowles Chapel Church

Chapter 6

The West Harpeth River

The West Harpeth River has its beginnings down to the east of the Lewisburg Pike on the northern slope of the Duck River Ridge, that long spine that separates the watershed areas of the Harpeth and Duck Rivers. The headwaters of the West Harpeth are made up of several small intermittent streams that finally come together in the vicinity of the Lewisburg Pike. At one point in this area, one of the streams leading eventually into the West Harpeth flows to the west within 1000 feet of a northeastern flowing tributary to Starnes Creek which flows into the Big Harpeth. Thus waters originating in the same small area of a few hundred square feet flow off in their separate ways for miles before ever being rejoined when the two rivers at last meet further to the north.

Passing under the Lewisburg Pike, the West Harpeth passes the New Hope Church. This church, one of the oldest Presbyterian congregations in this part of the country was founded in 1806 when this section was still nothing more than wilderness. Flowing northwestward from here, the river flows under the bridge carrying I-65 and behind Cowles Chapel, another old church of the area. Just beyond here it receives the waters of Kennedy Branch. Continuing its northwestwardly journey the West Harpeth flows under Highway 31 about three miles north of Thompson's Station, then under the Louisville and Nashville Railroad Line.

One of the Confederacy's better displays of strategy took place at Thompson's Station on March 5, 1863, under the leadership of Generals Earl Van Dorn and Nathan Bedford Forrest. Van Dorn, who had only arrived in Middle Tennessee the month before, and Forrest headed off a large Union contingent headed south from Franklin. Two Confederate brigades kept the Union troops busy on the front while Forrest slipped around the back in order to cut off any retreat to Franklin. It was during this action that Forrest personally took the Union commander, Colonel John Coburn of the 33rd Indiana, prisoner. Over twelve hundred other prisoners were taken by the Confederacy that day and their only losses were thirty killed and twenty-five wounded. Sometime during the fierce fighting a young local girl, Alice Thompson, ran into the thick of battle and took the place of one of the Confederate color bearers.

One of the sadder aspects of this battle was that General Forrest's favorite horse, Roderick, was mortally wounded in the thick of the conflict. Roderick was wounded during a critical charge and Forrest dispatched his favorite steed to the rear under the charge of his son, William Forrest. Taking William's horse as a replacement, the General pressed on into combat. Roderick, in the meantime, heard his master's voice calling out commands in the distance and set off in that direction to find him. In his attempt to locate his master, Roderick was wounded for a fourth time and upon reaching Forrest was in a very bad condition. Eyewitness reports indicate that Forrest hugged his beloved friend and burst into tears before pursuing the battle to its successful end. Shortly afterwards, Roderick died and was later buried on the battlefield. For years afterwards General Forrest's memories of this favorite stallion brought tears to his eyes.

By the time the West Harpeth passes under Highway 31 and the railroad, it is a sizable stream. Continuing on to Carter's Creek Pike from here and then to Highway 96 it picks up the waters of Polk Creek along the way. Just prior to going under old Highway 96, the West Harpeth receives the waters of Murfree's Fork. This stream, one of the largest tributaries to the West Harpeth, has its beginnings in the vicinity of Thompson's Station. Murfree's Fork starts out its journey to the south of the West Harpeth, but it flows in generally the same direction. By the time it collects the waters of Cayce Branch, it is already a fair sized creek.

Up Cayce Branch a few hundred yards from its confluence with Murfree's Branch lies Cayce Springs. Here is the site of a large resort hotel that was extremely popular during the last century. The hotel burned around 1890 and there is no trace of it at the present time. The springs are still active though, but they lie some distance from the road and are inaccessible to the general viewer.

Murfree's Fork and the West Prong of Murfree's Fork, two distinct streams, meet about two miles north of the Burwood Community and from this point the stream is known as Murfree's Fork for the rest of its journey to the West Harpeth. Colonel Hardee Murfree, who lent his name to the creek as well as to Murfreesboro, Tennessee, settled along Murfree's Fork back in the early 1800's. Before his death in 1809 Mur-

17. Iron Bridge over the West Harpeth

free, who hailed from North Carolina and for whose father the town of Murfreesboro, North Carolina was named, owned over 40,000 acres of Middle Tennessee land. It took a special commission set up by the Williamson County Court to settle Colonel Murfree's estate after his death. In addition to his vast land holdings Colonel Murfree left posterity with something far more valuable. His great-granddaughter was Mary Noailles Murfree. Miss Murfree, known for years in literary circles by her pseudonym of Charles Egbert Craddock, was responsible for the authorship of some twenty-five books over her long writing

18. Union Church at Leiper's Fork

career. Her works centered around the rugged mountain people of
Tennessee. One of them, *In the Tennessee Mountains,* is the only one
still in print, having recently been revived by the University of Tennessee
Press. At one time Miss Murfree lived in Nashville on Vauxhall Place.
This home, on what is now Ninth Avenue South, housed the Downtown
American Legion Post until it was razed in early 1971.

Shortly after passing beneath old Highway 96 the West Harpeth receives the waters of another of its larger tributaries, Leiper's Fork. Formed by the joining of Boston Branch and Robinson Branch just to the south of Boston, Leiper's Fork flows north until it receives the waters of Garrison Creek from the west. This creek is important in that it served as the southern terminus of the so-called Government Road of the Natchez Trace as explained in more detail in another chapter.

Garrison Creek has its beginnings near the Bending Chestnut community, presently characterized by a general store and the schoolhouse. Legend has it that the Indians used to take a sapling tree and bend it over till its top touched the ground. The tree would then be bound in this position and through the years would grow into old age in this bent position. One huge chestnut tree is said to have survived in this fashion on the school grounds for many years and this is how the community of Bending Chestnut received its name.

After receiving Garrison Creek, Leiper's Fork flows on generally northeastward till it reaches the town of Hillsboro, or as it is known today, Leiper's Fork. The town, Leiper's Fork, was named after the creek, Leiper's Fork, when the Post Office Department refused to have two towns in the same state with the same name, Hillsboro. (The other Hillsboro is in Coffee County on Highway 41.) Since the creek running through the town was called Leiper's Fork, it was only appropriate to call the town accordingly.

The origin of the name Leiper's Fork for the creek, however, is a different matter. This little stream received its name after Captain James Leiper, or Leeper as it is sometimes spelled. Leeper was one of the first settlers at Nashboro, and he and his bride, Susan Drake, were the first couple to be married in this settlement. This event took place in 1780, the first wedding west of the Cumberland Mountains, with none other than General James Robertson performing the ceremony.

Leeper, one of the signers of the Cumberland Compact, had explored the area around Leiper's Fork, but had never settled there. Indeed, he never lived outside the fort during his brief sojourn in Middle Tennessee. On April 2, 1781 while Fort Nashboro was being beseiged, he and several others were cut off from the fort while pursuing Indians. This was the battle in which Mrs. Robertson turned loose the dogs on the Indians. It was too late however, because Leeper and one of the Buchanans were killed in the fight. Ironically Leeper's young wife died accidently just three years later leaving a small daughter who had been born three months after Leeper's death.

Leeper is honored elsewhere than having a stream and town in Williamson County named after him. He is commemorated at Fort

Nashboro by a plaque which was dedicated in May, 1935. This plaque reads:

> "In memory of Captain James Leeper. His marriage was the first solemnized in the settlement. He was mortally wounded in the Battle of the Bluff, April 2, 1781."

The community of Leiper's Fork contains what is thought to be the oldest Church of Christ congregation in the entire South, south of Nashville. Formed in 1830 by two former Baptist ministers, this congregation was housed in the building called Union Church, which was built in 1815 and which originally housed several different denominations. The original Union Church building was torn down in 1845 and another structure was built in its place. This later building, like its predecessor, housed congregations from several denominations, specifically, "Baptists, Methodists, Cumberland Presbyterians, and Christians." These four faiths swapped Sundays with each other for thirty-two years until 1877 when the Baptists, Methodists, and Presbyterians sold out to the Church of Christ. The church was repaired at that time and it is this structure that can be seen serving as the center part of the building today.

Just beyond the town, Leiper's Fork passes under old Highway 96 and flows about another mile before releasing its waters to the West Harpeth River. The distance between old Highway 96 and new Highway 96 is less than four miles and the West Harpeth River flows generally northeastward for most of this distance. During most of the journey the river keeps pace generally with the Natchez Trace Road or Government Road to the west. Flowing under Boyd Mill Pike the river continues on past the community of Bingham, named after the family of the same name who inhabited these parts for years. Continuing a little further northward the river then flows under the bridge carrying new Highway 96, connecting Franklin with Linton.

Just after the West Harpeth flows under new Highway 96, it begins the final stage of its journey to its meeting with the Big Harpeth some three and a half miles away. Here at a point on the east bank of the river and just off the new highway lies the beautiful brick home built during the Civil War by Fielding Glass. This home, known in those days as "Locust Hill", was started in 1849 but construction had to be halted during the Civil War. The bricks in this house were all made right on the place. When constructed, the home faced the Old Charlotte Road

19. Deserted Store on Old Hillsboro Road

which connected Franklin with what is now Highway 100 and beyond. With the new construction however, and due to the fact that the bridge over the West Harpeth on Old Charlotte Road has been destroyed by the phosphate trucks which regularly haul away this valuable mineral from the ground in these parts, the approach to the old home is now from new Highway 96.

On the original property, but now on the south side of new Highway 96 between it and Boyd Mill Pike, lie two Indian Mounds in an extremely good state of repair. These mounds, judging from their present size and shape, were most likely built by the same people who built so many other complexes along the valley of the Harpeth. Tradition has it that the Smithsonian Institution dug into the mounds, but I can find no documentation relating to this fact.

Beyond the original Glass estate, now owned by Mrs. Hugh Channell, the great-grand-daughter of the home's builder, the West Harpeth continues its northward journey. On its west bank, just about one mile from its intersection with new Highway 96 lies "Walnut Hill". This antebellum mansion was built by Nicholas "Bigbee" Perkins for his daughter, Sarah, upon her marriage. Built in 1835, this home was the largest of all the Perkins homes which Nicholas built for his children, and even bigger than his own home place several miles away, "Montpier".

Walnut Hill suffered extreme damage in 1920 when a cyclone came through these parts and apparently completely destroyed the four columns in the front of the house. How the wind, even with cyclonic velocity, could have moved columns thirty feet tall and three feet in diameter is a mystery. An even bigger mystery is what happened to the columns after they were blown down. Tradition has it that they were never seen again.

The restoration of this home began upon the purchase of it by Mr. and Mrs. Claude Callicott. They did a beautiful job and today as one drives along Old Hillsboro Road, the mansion is visible through the trees to the east, its gleaming columns once again standing proud and erect much as they did, we suspect, over one hundred years ago.

20. Indian Mound on the West Harpeth

Passing "Walnut Hill", the West Harpeth makes its final run to its rendevous with the Harpeth. At this confluence of the two rivers stands yet another beautiful home. "Meeting of the Waters" is as charming a home as the lovely name used to describe it. Oldest of all the lovely homes which are so indigenous to the valley of the West Harpeth River, "Meeting of the Waters" was built around 1800 by Thomas Harden Perkins, the father-in-law of "Bigbee". "Bigbee", of whom more will be said later, married Thomas Harden's daughter, Mary, when he was twenty-nine and she was only fourteen. Some of the children of this union are whom some of the homes in this valley were built for, the existing one being "Walnut Hill", already mentioned. "Meeting of the Waters", presently owned and occupied by Mrs. Sam Woolwine and her sisters, Mrs. Lester Carroll, Jr. and Mrs. Perkins Trousdale, stands across the Del Rio Pike from the original Perkins' cemetery in which Nicholas "Bigbee" is buried. In later years "Meeting of the Waters" came into the possession of one of "Bigbee's" sons, Nicholas Edwin Perkins. Edwin's wife was a granddaughter of Abram Maury, one of the founders of Franklin and kinsman of Matthew Fontaine Maury.

To the west of "Meeting of the Waters" lies the site of another Perkins home, this one built for one of his sons. "Forest Home" laid on

21. Old Grocery Store at Forest Home

22. Meeting of the Waters

what is now the corner of the Old Natchez Trace and the Old Hillsboro Road. It burned in later years and no trace of it remains now except for the name of the little settlement which built up around· it and which is marked now by two deserted stores.

And so this lovely river, the only one of the Harpeths to have its source, its mouth, and its entire length totally in Williamson County, comes to an end. Killebrew has already been cited for his praise of the Little Harpeth River, pointing out that some of the finer country residences in the area lay in the valley of that stream. I daresay an equivalent has been found in the valley of the West Harpeth, with "Locust Hill", "Walnut Hill", and "Meeting of the Waters" all gracing the countryside today, and the ghost of "Forest Home" looming over the valley echoing the yester-years of history.

Chapter 7

The

Harpeth River

If you follow State Highway 99 from Eagleville to the community of
Rockvale in Rutherford County, you will pass over several tiny intermittent streams. Most of these are so small that they simply go under the
road through culverts since they aren't large enough to merit a bridge.
These streams all begin just a little way to the south of the highway,
and after they independently go under it, they all meet not too far to
the north to form the Harpeth River.

When looking at these tiny creeks in the summer, when for long
periods of time they are completely dry, it is hard to conceive that this
is the same river which, further downstream along its 117 mile journey
to the Cumberland, can be so furious during the winter and spring
rains. For indeed the Harpeth can be furious in flood stage. Just about
every winter the Harpeth, unchecked anywhere along its entire length
or along any of its tributaries, leaves its banks as it sends its muddy,
driftwood laden waters all over the surrounding country-side. Engulfing
farmlands and closing passage on roads during these tirades the mighty
Harpeth finally takes control of itself and quietens down as the flood
waters pass.

The town of Eagleville, which is situated near the area in which all
of the tributary branches to the Harpeth are located, is one of the oldest
settlements in Rutherford County. It lies in the extreme southwest portion of the county, just over the Williamson County border. The folks
around Eagleville had a real scare back before the turn of the century
in 1898 when a rash of grave robberies began. It wasn't long until tales
of ghosts began circulating among the folks in town, and before the
stories got warm, three bodies turned up missing from the local grave-

yard. When the news of the body-snatching arrived in Nashville, Governor Bob Taylor activated the militia and had them make a door to door search of all the medical schools and facilities in Nashville.

Turning up nothing in the capital city, the search for the missing bodies was continued by a private detective who some time later located two of the corpses in Burlington, Vermont. These two bodies were packed in a crate marked "Books". Some of the ghoulish atmosphere was dismissed then, and at last the true facts came to light. It appears that a local doctor had been offered a deal by a big eastern outfit to acquire bodies for scholastic autopsy use. He received forty-five dollars each for these bodies, and apparently had just begun to get serious with this business when he got caught.

At the time the doctor was arrested, he could be tried on nothing more than a misdemeanor charge, since the law against grave robbing called for nothing more than that. Consequently he got off with the workhouse and a $150 fine. The incident caused such a furor, however, that the following year, 1899, the Tennessee Legislature passed a law making it a felony, and punishable by a prison sentence of two to five years, to rob graves of bodies for the purpose of selling them for instructional purposes.

By the time the various little creeks that form the headwaters of the Harpeth come together north of Highway 99, the result is a sizable stream. At it flows under U. S. Highway 41A, still in Rutherford County, it is still small but by that time it does carry water the year around. A little further from here it meets with the Williamson County border about two miles south of the Kirkland community. It then follows the county line in a northerly direction for a little over a mile before entering Williamson County in its entirety. About a mile further north from here, it goes under U. S. Highway 31A between College Grove and Kirkland.

One of College Grove's most prosperous landowners in the middle 1800's was William Demonbreun. He moved to this area from Davidson County and became a very wealthy planter and slave owner. Probably better known than William, however, was his father. The elder Demonbreun, Timothy, is best known locally for having lived in a cave in the bluffs of the Cumberland River above Nashville for a period of time before Nashville was actually settled by English speaking people. Timothy was from Quebec and he had fought with the French Army in Canada during the French and Indian War. There, in 1759 as a

Captain, he took part in the Battle of Quebec which saw the French severely defeated by the British. Still a young man after the war was over, he journeyed to the Cumberland country and settled temporarily in the cave on the bluffs above the Cumberland River. Timothy located permanently in Nashville sometimes later and William was born in Nashville in 1794. He was a long-time resident of the College Grove area, dying in 1870.

Leaving this vicinity, the Harpeth continues its ever onward, north-westward journey toward Franklin. Passing under the eastern branch of the Louisville and Nashville Railroad connecting Brentwood with Athens, Alabama, the big river picks up the waters of Nelson Creek a little farther along. Going on further it receives Arrington Creek from the north-east and further still, Starnes Creek from the south. Finally passing under Interstate 65, the Harpeth pulls up beside the Lewisburg Pike and follows it into Franklin.

As the Harpeth approaches Franklin from the southeast it passes the area of a once extensive Indian town. This town was situated on the west bank of the Harpeth between it and what is now the Lewisburg Pike. As well as I can determine there are no remains of this site in existence, having been destroyed over the years by the farmer's plow. In its prime, however, it was one of the largest such towns on the Harpeth.

Joseph Jones explored this area in the 1860's and at that time many

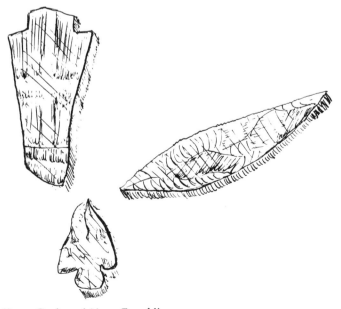

23. Artifacts Gathered Near Franklin

of the remains were still in existence. Jones estimated that the earthwork surrounding the town was 3800 feet long and that it enclosed at
least 32 acres. Protected on one side by the bluffs of the Harpeth River,
the town was surrounded on the other three sides by this earthwork
which in all likelihood was crowned by a wooden stockade. There were
nine mounds within the stockade, and by the time Jones explored them,
the elements had reduced all of them in size. Even though smaller than
they once were, the largest one still measured 230 feet by 110 feet and
stood 16 feet tall. Some of the mounds had apparently been used for
ceremonial purposes, while others contained burials.

In one of the burial mounds, Jones found what he described as a
"Stone Sword". This remarkable implement, which in reality was probably a ceremonial piece, was finely chipped from one piece of flint and
measured 22 inches in length. In his description of this site Jones quickly
added that, "This appears to be the largest and most perfect chipped
stone implement of this kind ever discovered either in America or elsewhere." In another reference to this implement Jones indicated, "During
the summer of 1870, I carefully examined the collections of antiquities
in the museum of Paris, London, Liverpool, Cambridge, Oxford, and
Edinburgh, but found no stone implement equalling in size and per-
fection the "Stone Sword" just described . . ."

In another grave were found four thin copper plates with a cross in
the middle of each. Each plate had a small hole in one end which led
Jones to believe that they were probably worn as necklaces. The presence of these "necklaces" of copper, along with sea shells in these
burials would indicate that there was quite a bit of trade going on in this
section of the country at that time. This fact did not escape the keen
eye of Dr. Jones, who also found fragments of obsidian and mica,
neither of which are naturally found in the area. With his usual insight
he commented upon this observation by saying.

> "It is evident, from the following observations, that the stone im-
> plements from the ancient earthwork on the banks of the Big
> Harpeth River were formed of various kinds of stone which are
> unknown in this section of North America. . . . It is probable that
> the places whence some of these materials were obtained were
> from 300 to 2000 miles distant; and the conclusion is reached that
> either these implements were obtained during the migrations of the
> race from distant regions, during long hunting and war expeditions,
> or by barter from surrounding nations."

A little way beyond the old Indian town, and lying on the opposite
bank of the Harpeth, once stood Fort Granger. Named for its Com-

manding Officer, General Gordon Granger, this fort was built in 1862 and served as a federal advance post. The perimeter of the fort was some 800-900 feet long, and at its height of occupation it housed 8,500 men and boasted 24 artillery pieces. The fort was dismantled some time prior to the Battle of Franklin. Nevertheless, the Federals took advantage of the fort's strategic position during the conflict, and re-fortified it with cannon, which were used to fire upon the Confederate forces to the south.

The Battle of Franklin has probably had as much written about it as any other battle that took place during the Civil War. This conflict could easily be called the most unnecessary battle of the War. No important ground was lost or taken. No strategic towns were captured—the whole battle was nothing more than a delaying action for the Federals who couldn't get to Nashville fast enough, and a "grudge" battle on the part of the Confederates who were so successfully eluded by the Federals the night before at Spring Hill. While the present Federal government has never given recognition to the Battle of Franklin as being a battle of extreme importance, it was one of national interest both in the effects it had on the later Battle of Nashville and in the fact that so many general officers of the Confederacy were killed or otherwise immobilized there.

The Battle of Franklin was fought on November 30, 1864. The opponents were Generals John B. Hood of the Confederacy and John M. Schofield of the Union Army. Hood was only 33 at the time and Schofield was about the same age. Both were West Point graduates and were classmates while there. Hood had only recently received total command of the Army of Tennessee, having replaced General Joseph E. Johnston. He had come a long way from the rank of First Lieutenant in the U. S. Army in Texas in 1861 to the complete command of the Department of Tennessee just three years later. He had suffered coming this far however. He had no use of his left arm, and his right leg had been amputated due to battle injuries.

In the early fall of 1864, after Atlanta had fallen to the Union Army and Sherman was free to negotiate any place that he wanted to, Hood came up with the idea of marching on Nashville, and in so doing destroyed the Nashville and Chattanooga Railroad which was Sherman's supply line. Schofield, in the meantime, convinced Sherman that if Hood did indeed cross over into Tennessee with the idea in mind of taking Nashville, that General George H. Thomas who was occupying Nashville at the time could not hold out against the Confederate foe. Sherman therefore dispatched Schofield and his Twenty-third Corps to Nashville to assist General Thomas in the defense of the city.

November 29 saw both armies gathered around Spring Hill, Tennessee. The next morning, however, Hood awoke to find that Schofield's entire corps had slipped through the Confederate lines and was on its way to Franklin. Schofield was planning to keep his troops on the move until they reached Nashville, but Hood was so infuriated at the situation that he force marched his men, and as the evening of the 30th began to draw to a close, the Confederate forces were on the outskirts of Franklin. Schofield, having already realized that he could never make it to Nashville in one trip, had already raised fortifications and taken strategic positions along the south side of the town. The fortifications were strongest along the gap where the Columbia Pike came through, and it was in this area around the Carter House that some of the fiercest fighting took place.

The Confederate Army, not far behind, drew up to the south of Franklin and after surveying the situation, Hood made the decision to go into battle against the advice of Generals Cheatham and Forrest. Hood based his decision on the premise that he should attack before Schofield could get too deeply entrenched. Unbeknowing to him, however, Schofield was already firmly entrenched and in excellent fighting position. Not waiting for his artillery or even other contingents of his infantry, Hood ordered the attack at four o'clock in the afternoon.

At one point the Federal line was broken through but a reserve force of Union troops drove the charge back and closed the line. The fighting was furious and continued into the night. And then the Union guns fell silent. Schofield had done it again. He had crossed the Harpeth River on the north side of Franklin and slipped away with his entire army to Nashville.

The official casualty figures for the Confederacy were 6,202 dead and wounded out of a total force of 29,250 men. The Union Army suffered 2,326 casualties but about 1,000 of these were prisoners. Considering these rather high casualty figures, especially those in Hood's army, this battle has been called one of the bloodiest engagements of the entire Civil War. Of the 6000 plus casualties on the Confederate side, an almost unbelievable twelve of these were general officers. Killed in the conflict were Generals P. R. Cleburne, S. R. Gist, H. B. Granbury, John Adams, and O. F. Stradl. Wounded were Generals John C. Carter, John C. Brown, A. M. Manigault, William A. Quarles, F. M. Cockrell, and T. M. Scott. General George W. Gordon was captured.

Most battles have a clear cut victor, but Franklin does not. Both sides claimed victory, but neither really won it. As Stanley Horn points out so succinctly in his book, *Tennessee's War*, victory could hardly be claimed by Schofield since he retreated from a position that he was supposed to hold for three days after only a few hours of fighting. On the other hand victories are hard to claim when they involve a twenty per-cent casualty rate, which is what Hood suffered.

One of the saddest aspects of the entire engagement at Franklin was the fact that young Theodoric Carter—better known as Tod, son of the owner of the Carter House—lost his life within mere yards of his own home. Tod was the second oldest of the three surviving Carter sons and along with his other two brothers, Moscow and Francis, had enlisted in the Confederate Army in May, 1861, at Franklin. Tod was only 24 at the time of the Battle of Franklin, but had already reached the rank of Captain on the staff of General Thomas Benton Smith.

One of the soldiers brought the news to the Carter family, still in the basement of the house where they had sought refuge from the after-noon's fighting, that young Tod had fallen on the field of battle. Mem-bers of the family went out after the fighting had ceased and bore back

24. The Confederate Cemetery at Franklin

his body to the homeplace he had not seen for two years. Tod Carter was so near, yet so far. He was destined never to see his home again in life, but in death he was laid in the yard where he had spent his happy childhood moments in those careless days of long ago in the valley of the Harpeth.

Lying a short distance from where the fiercest fighting at Franklin took place lies "Carnton". This beautiful anti-bellum mansion just off the Lewisburg Pike was the home of Colonel John McGavock. The morning after the battle found all five of the Confederate generals who lost their lives in the conflict laid out on the porch at "Carnton". McGavock donated some adjoining property for use as a cemetery for those who fell at Franklin. The generals were buried elsewhere, but the cemetery contains the bodies of 1496 other veterans of the war.

The cemetery contains burials representing most of the Confederate States plus some border states. The November 17, 1866 issue of the *Harper's Weekly* was very complimentary of it, giving the following remarks along with an engraving:

> "We give herewith a view of the Confederate Cemetery at Franklin, Tennessee—the scene, as our readers remember, of the Battle between General Schofield and the rebels under General Hood, a little before the great and decisive Battle of Nashville. The Cemetery is beautifully situated, about a mile southeast of Franklin, on the farm of Colonel John McGavock. It contains 1485 graves, and in its general appearance is an improvement upon some of the National Cemeteries which we have had occasion to illustrate."

The discrepancy in the number of burials shown in *Harper's* and the number actually buried there today probably lies in the fact that several additional veterans were buried at Franklin in later years after the war.

Today the cemetery is a very quiet, serene place. Being well off the main highway, it lies snuggled among some very old and stately cedar trees. It is a long narrow piece of ground, surrounded by a wrought iron fence. Off to the right, as one stands looking at the cemetery from the front, lies "Carnton" about two hundred yards away and appearing as lovely today as it must have one hundred years ago.

Walking toward the back of the cemetery down the center row, one passes to the right and left the markers denoting the state of the Confederacy represented and the number of men from that state who lost their lives at Franklin. Small square stones with the initials of the person buried are the only evidences of burials with the exception of some larger stones here and there with full information on them which were apparently placed later by family members. In addition to the state groupings there is a section of unknowns. In the very rear of the cemetery are the McGavock family burials containing the graves of various members of the household of "Carnton."

How costly the battle was in terms of men lost. How often this same scene must have been repeated during the long dark days of the war. Today, Franklin; tomorrow, Nashville. Where next? Well, there wasn't long to go. If the boys who died at Franklin could have held out a little longer, it would have all been over in a few short months. For then in April of the following year, 1865, at a little place in Virginia called Appomatox Court House the curtain would finally fall. When Lee and Grant stepped out on the porch of the Mc-Lean House and announced it was all over, there must have been a sigh of relief among the troops on both sides. But it was four months too late for the boys buried at Franklin.

Before leaving Franklin the Harpeth passes under the western branch of the L & N Railroad connecting Brentwood and Athens, Alabama. Then it goes under the Franklin-Nashville Road, Highway 31. Spencer Creek adds its contribution to the river a little further on and then, picking up strength all the time, the Harpeth passes beneath Highway 431, the Hillsboro Road.

Not too far from the Harpeth as it winds itself around to form Walker's Bend lies "River Grange," the home of Mr. and Mrs. Livingfield More. This fine old home was built by Nicholas Tate Perkins in the early 1800's. Nicholas Tate Perkins is not to be confused with Nicholas "Bigbee" Perkins about whom we have already read and will have more to say later. The men were cousins however, and Nicholas Tate married Nicholas "Bigbee's" sister. Nicholas Tate Perkins was born in North Carolina in 1767. He married Anne Perkins, his cousin, who was born in 1770. Nicholas Tate was a leading citizen of Williamson County and served in the State Senate.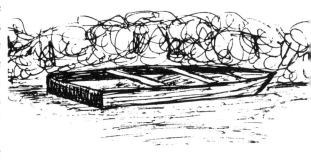

"River Grange" in those days was called "Poplar Grove" because of the abundance of yellow poplar trees which grew about the home site. The home stands on ground that was part of an original land grant to a Mr. Stewart in 1793. Stewart's son sold the land to Nicholas Tate Perkins in 1802, and the house was built shortly thereafter. In later years the house and land was sold out of the Perkins' hands to Otey Walker, and it was from this Walker that the land received the name Walker's Bend.

To the west of "Poplar Grove" lies another fine old home built by Nicholas Tate Perkins. Facing Del Rio Pike about midway between "Poplar Grove" and "Meeting of the Waters" is the home of Mr. James

Buford. The period of this fine old home can be surmised by comparing the architecture of it and the other Perkins' homes. It is quite obvious that they were built during the same time, and they are all truly fine old homes.

After leaving Walker's Bend the Harpeth winds around to "Meeting of the Waters" where it receives the West Harpeth River from the south. Passing near the village of Forest Home, the river winds around Lumsden Bend, past Old Town. Following the general direction of the Natchez Trace Road for some time, the Harpeth finally tires of this game and heads off into Sawyer Bend. Flowing under the old iron bridge on Moran Road the river flows into Pierce Bend before passing the site of the old covered Union Bridge.

The original bridge at this point was built around 1840, but was destroyed during the Civil War. It was rebuilt in 1881 with a third stone pier in the middle of the river helping to hold the weight. It was known from this time on as the Union Bridge because of the financial "union" between Davidson and Williamson Counties in paying for the construction. A flood on February 13, 1948 washed away the entire structure leaving this part of the state with no covered bridges.

A loop around Hicks Bend carries the Harpeth out of Williamson County forever, but only after the Little Harpeth deposits its load into its larger brother on the Davidson-Williamson County line. Passing under Highway 100 the Harpeth flows into Beech Bend and here receives the waters from Trace Creek. This small stream has its beginnings south of here on Backbone Ridge. The proximity of the source of Trace Creek with the old, original Natchez Trace has earned it its name.

Beyond Beech Bend the Harpeth passes under the Old Harding Pike at Bellevue. The Old Harding Pike prior to the construction of Highway 100 was the only link Nashville had to the southwest. Coming out of Nashville as the Richland Pike, it ascended Nine Mile Hill, passed through Bellevue and went straight through to Pasquo and beyond. Even today, all along portions of Highway 70 between Nine Mile Hill and Bellevue, and on Highway 100 between Pasquo and Linton, there are several places where portions of the Old Harding Road can still be seen. Straighter road construction in later years has taken the curves out of the highways so that now, what were once sections of a winding road are now just mere cutoffs to the right or left of the main highway.

After playing hopscotch with Interstate 40 for a while the Harpeth arrives at Newsom's Station. At one time this magnificent mill and its associated dam was impressive indeed as they sat beside and astride the Big Harpeth. Built in 1862 by Jimmy Newsom, there's no telling how many thousands of pounds of meal this old place produced before

25. Newsom's Mill

falling into decay. The dam has broken now and stores no water behind it for power purposes. The mill itself is as substantial looking now as it ever was, however, being constructed of neat square-cut stones. Jimmy Newson wouldn't know the place now with Interstate 40 passing nearby and the dragstrip next door.

A little further downstream from Newsom's Station, the Harpeth leaves Davidson County. Entering Cheatham County southeast of Pegram, situated on the Nashville, Chattanooga and St. Louis Railway line, it swings around another bend before it comes to the place where it receives the waters of the last of its major tributaries, the South Harpeth River.

In this vicinity lies what is known as Buffalo Gap. Lying several river miles upstream from Mound Bottom, the Gap is visible today near the Kingston Springs exit on Interstate Highway 40. Buffalo Gap was recognized for what it was; i.e., a pass in the cliff through which the vast herds of buffalo passed, as far back as the early 1800's. Dr. Jones was aware of its presence and commented:

> "At Buffalo Gap, on the same stream, where the ancient trail of the buffalo is still distinct, a line of these animals is painted on the cliff of rocks which overhangs the river.
> The hollow formed by the projecting rocks at Buffalo Gap, on Big Harpeth, is capable of sheltering at least one thousand men, and it would appear that this was, in ancient times, a favorite resort of the Indian hunters."

The painting of the buffalo referred to in Jones' passage is barely visible today, having been chipped away by vandals. We can visualize some nameless hunter of a bygone age crouching in this place as he attempted to portray a scene that he had witnessed hundreds of times since boyhood. He could not remember how many thousands of animals that he had seen thunder through that pass. But today, he would capture on the rocks themselves for all time and for all people the scenes he had seen. So, bidding his family farewell for the day, he left his village early in the morning in order to finish his task and be home by nightfall. He might have come from Mound Bottom or any one of a half-dozen other villages strung up and down the river. In addition to his weapons, which were ever present, he carried with him on this trip his paints. Made out of various natural occuring commodities depending on the color desired, his paint was probably mixed with animal grease for consistency. Picking a good protected spot in which to paint, his finished product was the line of buffalo that, up until a few years ago, could still be seen.

This exercise in pictorial representation of a familiar scene could have been done for beauty's sake or for magical purposes. Perhaps the painted scene in this place could somehow insure for all time that the herds of buffalo would be numerous, and that they would always use this pass in their wanderings where the hunters could lie in wait for them. All too often a utilitarian use is put on primitive art such as the above. This may be true. But somehow I can't help but believe that these early inhabitants of the Harpeth Valley appreciated beauty for its own sake. Maybe this fellow just wanted to portray something as he had seen it and did so, hoping that other passer-bys would appreciate it too. Perhaps I'm too much of a romantic. Judge for yourself why the scene was painted. What once was there for all to see is now gone, however, and the scene as well as the artist is now unfortunately forgotten.

Leaving the Buffalo Gap area the Harpeth passes through Kingston Springs. Here was another large resort hotel, at one time extremely popular for its mineral waters. Unlike the hotels at Fernvale and Cayce Springs, however, the one at Kingston Springs is still standing. The hotel and its cottages lie south of Kingston Springs proper and on the west side of the road leading from the Interstate 40 exit.

26. Rock Painting at Buffalo Gap

27. Ancient Petroglyph Above Mound Bottom

Passing Kingston Springs the Harpeth picks up the waters of Turn-bull Creek, and in so doing it picks up its first waters from Dickson County. Rolling along at a more rapid pace now, the Harpeth approaches Mound Bottom. As the river reaches Highway 70, the Great Mound Division of this ancient Indian town lies off to the left. Flowing a little further the river then goes into the tight bend of the river known properly as "Mound Bottom". It was in this bend that laid the other half of the ancient town. Both phases of Mound Bottom Town are investigated at fuller length in a later chapter.

High above the Harpeth on the steep cliff which overhangs the Mound Bottom Division of the aforementioned town is a petroglyph inscribed in the rocks. Lying on the north side of the bend of the river, the petroglyph depicts what appears to be a baton. It measures about 14 inches in length, and one can only guess as to its original meaning and under what circumstances some unknown sculptor chipped away at this rock in order to give us the engraving we see today.

Petroglyphs are fairly common in North America, and have long been recognized as a mode of expression by the native inhabitants. The *Handbook of American Indians,* published by the Bureau of American Ethnology has this to say of petroglyphs:

"The form of picture writing known as the petroglyph is of world-wide distribution and is common over most of North America. Petroglyphs may be pecked or incised, or painted; occasionally they are rendered both permanent and conspicuous by being first incised and then painted. They appear on sea-worn boulders, on glacier-polished rocks, on canyon cliffs, and within caves . . . petroglyphs of the incised form are common in the N., while colored ones are more numerous in the S. . . ."

At another place the *Handbook* states:

"When interrogated, modern Indians often disclaim knowledge of or interest in the origin and significance of the petroglyphs, and often explain them as the work of supernatural beings, which explanation in the minds of many invests them with still deeper mystery. Beyond the fact that by habits of thought and training the Indian may be presumed to be in closer touch with the glyph maker than the more civilized investigator, the Indian is no better qualified to interpret petroglyphs than the latter, and in many respects, indeed, is far less qualified, even though the rock pictures may have been made by his forebearers."

From the above, even though these passages are referring to petro-glyphs in general, it is apparent that our Mound Bottom engraving is of extreme antiquity. It is most likely that this feature was created during the time that Mound Bottom was in its zenith.

Flowing along further now the Harpeth comes into the area known as "The Narrows". Down through the years one name above all others has been associated with this length of the Harpeth—that of Montgomery Bell. If a poll had been taken in the early 19th century in an effort to name "the most successful businessman of Dickson County", Montgomery Bell would surely have been named. His story in the Tennessee country is one of overwhelming success in his profession, and his name lives on today throughout the area in the presence of Montgomery Bell Academy. This school for boys in Nashville is one of the finest private schools in the South, and it has its beginnings in the fund set aside by Montgomery Bell for its formation.

Montgomery Bell was born in Chester County, Pennsylvania, in 1769. He moved south at an early age, and after a brief sojourn in Kentucky, he wound up at the Cumberland Iron Works in Dickson County, Tennessee. This furnace, near the present town of Cumberland Furnace, was established in 1793 by James Robertson, co-founder of Nashville. The section of country that this area lies in, comprising what today would be known as Western Middle Tennessee, was found early to be very rich in iron ore. It probably would not be classified as such today with the mining being done with giant steam shovels capable of gulping up several tons of ore at a single bite. But in those older days when it probably took all week to extract the same amount of ore from the earth that today takes at the most several minutes, this entire section was indeed a rich one and a welcome source of raw material for farm and other metal implements to the new settlers.

Remember that this entire expanse of land west of the Appalachian Mountains was only seriously beginning to be explored and settled by the late 18th century. Nashboro, now Nashville, was settled in 1780 and at the time constituted the westernmost English speaking settlement in the old southwest. Thus it was that any iron implements that these early pioneers had in this, their new home, consisted only of those items that were brought with them from the Wautauga settlements. There must have been a great demand for new supplies of iron implements, not only cooking gear, but also farm and wood-working tools, and the demand either went unsatisfied or the tools were brought in from the East. Demands grew and grew and importation from the East remained extremely timely and dangerous, so that the only other alternative to the problem was a home-made solution—manufacture of the needed implements right here where the demand was.

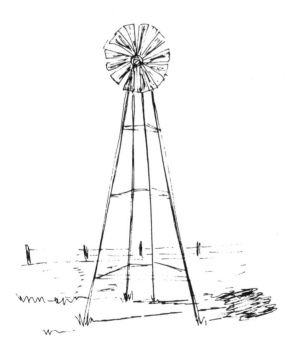

We can only guess the excitement of the unknown person who first discovered that there was iron in the hills about Middle Tennessee. Not only was there iron here; it was here in such quantities that would make it a profitable endeavor for someone to open up a furnace and provide iron for the needs of the growing population of the Cumberland Country.

This, then, provided the backdrop upon which James Robertson founded his iron furnace in Dickson County, even though Dickson County itself had not been officially established at that time. Robertson had varied interests throughout his career in Middle Tennessee. He was leader, farmer, surveyor, and soldier all rolled up into one. Hence when he established his iron smelter at Cumberland Furnace, his other activities kept him from devoting more than cursory participation in its proper management. Consequently the furnace, under Robertson's direction, was never brought up to its full potential. Cumberland Furnace was the very first iron smelter in Middle Tennessee and only the second one in the entire state. We can imagine, therefore, the good business that was done at this smelter since it, even at limited production, was depended upon for supplying iron for the entire needs of all the area.

Montgomery Bell served his apprenticeship under Robertson at the Cumberland Iron Works. Then, in 1804, he bought out Robertson for

$16,000 and became the sole owner of the furnace. Knowing full well that the potentialities of the furnace were not being taken advantage of, Bell within a very short period increased production of pig iron by two fold, then three fold, until finally just one year later his production had outrun Robertson's by several hundred per cent. So greatly did Bell increase his total output at the forge that it is said that practically the entire supply of cannon balls used by the Americans in the War of 1812 were moulded at the Cumberland Iron Works. They were shipped down the Cumberland River to the Ohio, down the Ohio to the Mississippi, and then down the Mississippi to the Gulf at New Orleans.

The "Yankee ingenuity" in Montgomery Bell was not satisfied with the mere expansion of iron production at this one forge. It was not enough. If one furnace could be developed to yield as much iron as Cumberland Furnace, then several more could yield many fold the annual production. So, Bell expanded his holdings and his forges. Before he was through he had spent over $150,000 for real estate alone in the Middle Tennessee area. He opened one forge after another until he could list the following as full, operative enterprises:

Carroll Furnace on the Cumberland River
Upper Forge on Jones Creek
Bellevue Forge on Jones Creek
Valley Forge on Jones Creek
White Bluff Forge on Turnbull Creek
Piney Furnace on Piney River
Worley Furnace—South of Dickson

Bell's pride and joy, however, was one not listed above. This was the Pattison (not Patterson as it is sometimes incorrectly spelled) Iron Works on the Harpeth River in what was to become Cheatham County. Named in honor of his mother, her maiden name being Pattison, this is the place where Bell built his home and lived until his death in 1855.

This section of the Harpeth River is full of meandering bends, and Bell was quick to see the potential that one of these bends offered him in the way of latent water power. As the Harpeth breaks out of Mound Bottom, the site of the ancient Mississippian Indian village referred to earlier, it runs for a way before snaking around to make another bend and head back in the same direction it just came from. This bend, appropriately named Bell's Bend, is a large one and at one point the waters of the Harpeth pass within 180 feet of the waters on the opposite side of the bend even though these waters are separated by five or six miles of river distance. Bell reasoned that since the levels of these two aspects of the same river differed by some fifteen feet, that if a tunnel could be constructed through the ridge separating the waters, then the water from

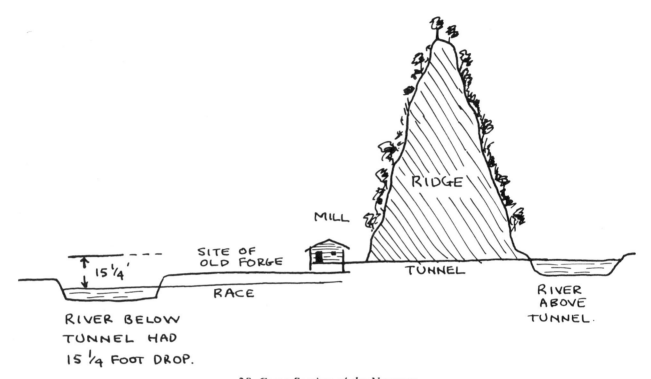

28. Cross-Section of the Narrows

the high side would rush through this tunnel to get to the low side with such velocity as to provide him with an excellent source of power. He couldn't have been more correct.

The tunnel was pushed through the solid rock of the dividing ridge by slave labor, and it is estimated that it took about a year's work at seven days a week to complete the task. When the job was done, the tunnel was sixteen feet wide and eight feet high. At the river's low stage it was capable of delivering 2,500 cubic feet of water through the tunnel per minute. When the construction was over, Bell had his Pattison Forge built on the downstream side of the tunnel and built a race in order to get the diverted water back into its original channel. This is the place known today as the Narrows of the Harpeth.

In addition to being the leading iron-master in this section of the country, Bell was also a large slave-holder. Of course, a large portion of his forge construction was carried about by slave labor necessitating a large number, at one time reaching about three hundred. At some point, however, Bell became a convert of the idea of freeing all the slaves and helping them return to Africa. This idea, popular in the period between 1820-1847, specifically called for the liberation of the

slaves so that they could be returned to Liberia, a state on the west
coast of Africa established with United States assistance largely for
this purpose. Bell presented the offer to his slaves and only about fifty
of them were interested in the idea. These fifty he assisted in getting to
Nashville, where they caught the boat which took them to New Orleans
and we suppose eventual freedom.

So, this Montgomery Bell was quite a fellow. In 1850 in London,
England, the product from his furnaces earned the prize, "The Best Iron
in the World." Just five years later, he died in his beloved home not far
from the Narrows of the Harpeth. One by one his furnaces fell into ruin
until at last they were all gone. In 1883 his Pattison Forge site, along
with 1840 acres of surrounding lands, were sold at public auction. This
ended the legend of Montgomery Bell, Iron Master of Tennessee.

29. Harris-Street Bridge

Further down the Harpeth several miles and again high up on the
cliffs above the river are some more petroglyphs. This place, opposite
from Corlew Bend, is called Paint Rock Bluff. It lies on the Dickson

County side of the river along that stretch that serves as a border between Dickson and Cheatham Counties. These petroglyphs are painted on the perpendicular side of the cliff and it is generally agreed by their looks and color that they represent the sun and the moon, and that these representations some 200 feet above the river and visible for several miles were somehow used in religious ceremonies. The "sun" is estimated to be about five feet across and the distance that the symbols lie below the overhang of the cliff makes it difficult to imagine how the primitive artist reached this place in order to paint these images.

That these ancient people on the Harpeth should worship the sun, moon, and other celestial bodies is not strange. As a matter of fact, many American Indian peoples worshipped the sun. The Toltecs, forerunners of the Aztecs in the Valley of Mexico, at Teotihuacan had giant pyramids constructed for the worship of these heavenly deities. The Temple of the Sun there rose 216 feet high and covered 10 acres of ground. Its sister Temple of the Moon was somewhat smaller. The Aztecs themselves were also avid sun-worshippers. Their sun-god demanded blood, and it was this belief that caused the Aztecs to take prisoners of so many of the enemy, in order to sacrifice them to the Sun. At specified times, the sacred procession would climb the stairway of the great pyramid and when all was ready would await the grand moment. Then, just as the morning sun peeked over the eastern horizon, the high priest would slash open the body of the victim and go into the cavity with his hand, pulling the still throbbing heart completely out of the body. Untold thousands died a similar death in order to appease the voracious appetite of the sun god.

Closer at home the Natchez Indians of Mississippi were also sun worshippers. Their society was broken down into castes, the highest of which, the nobles, were actually called "Suns". The principal chief himself was called the Great Sun. He was thought to be the younger brother of the Sun, and every morning would find him on the top of a large mound welcoming his older brother upon his arrival in the eastern sky and directing his journey across the skies by a wave of the arm from east to west.

What type of religious ceremonies took place in ancient times on the Harpeth River, we probably will never know. It is doubtful that any future archaeological evidence will ever be produced to fill in the gaps in our knowledge concerning this important facet of these people's lives. Possibly long processions of religious folk filed out of the stockade at Mound Bottom and followed the river the few miles down to Corlew Bend opposite Paint Rock Bluff. There they might have been met by other peoples from up and down the river, possibly from such places as

30. Swinging Bridge over the Harpeth

Old Town, Gordontown, and the Fewkes Site. After the usual amenities and renewal of old friendships, perhaps the principal chief of all the river towns gathered the individual chiefs and priests together and after instructing them in their individual duties, commenced the ceremonies. Perhaps the ceremony this time was being held in order to show to all the people the new symbols being painted on the side of the bluff in order to give the sun a partner in its vigil over the Harpeth River.

Several people are gathered together here and there, and there are mumblings among them as to how an additional symbol will be painted on the side of the bluff. The sun itself was painted some years ago, and no one here can remember under what circumstances this occurred. It looks to be a full one hundred feet from the top of the bluff down to the place where the painting will take place. The mumbling suddenly ceases as the principal chief now appears atop a platform on the river's edge. It is apparent that the crowd won't have to guess long as to how the task of painting on the bluff will be accomplished because the chief is now issuing his final instructions to four men, whom the people recognize as being the four most outstanding artisans of the valley. The chief and all his assistants, along with the priests and the four artisans, stand a long time looking at the bluffs. Then, suddenly among the roarings of a hundred drums and the cries of a thousand people, the four artisans each accompanied by a helper who carries his supplies, dash away from the platform. In twos, they run alongside the river, four of the men going off in opposite directions from the other four. About one hundred yards away from the platform, two of the men upstream and two downstream cross the river, while the remaining four continue. These four continue another hundred yards, and then they too make right angle turns into and across the river. The eight men are all obscured from sight now on the opposite side of the river as they all use different avenues of approach

31. Paint Rock Bluff

to the top of the cliff. Then suddenly, all eight men appear simultaneously on the bluff and the drums stop their beating and the crowd stops its howling.

For the next several hours the crowd below in Corlew's Bend stand in stark disbelief as the four artisans drop themselves on lines over the face of the cliff in order to perform the tedious task at hand. Having their paints passed to them from the top of the cliff by their four assistants, the artisans work for several hours before being hoisted up from their precarious perches high above the river. As the four regain their footing at the top, the crowd roars its approval and the drums begin their playing. When all have had a chance to see, the principal chief puts an end to the ceremony with a wave of his hand. The finished product on the cliff is the moon, little sister to the sun. Now, instead of just the sun which was painted at a time beyond the memory of this crowd, they have the moon to worship or adore as they wish.

The long trek home now begins for the hundreds of folks assembled in Corlew's Bend. This has indeed been a day that will long be remembered in the minds of all those who attended this ceremony. Next time, when the regular ceremonies take place, all present will remember how the fabulous work on the side of the cliff was accomplished.

The preceding is a flight into fantasy because no one really knows how the images on Paint Rock Bluff came to be there. They were there when the first whites came to the area, and like the numerous mounds and deserted villages, the Indians present in the area at that time disclaimed any knowledge whatsoever of where the images came from or by whom they were performed.

Here then, within seven air miles, are three examples of American Indian prehistoric art. The first, Buffalo Gap with its paintings, and the last, Paint Rock Bluff, with its images of the sun and the moon painted onto the sheer side of the cliff above the Harpeth, represent the painted version of the petroglyph. The second one, the baton carved into the rock above Mound Bottom, more accurately falls into the category of incised glyphs.

Time and the elements have worn heavily upon these art forms up and down the valley. Man himself has not helped any. Destructive as he always is, he has striven over the past century to destroy Paint Rock Bluff by gradually chipping away the face of the cliff with rifle fire, leaving the original paintings only mere outlines of what they must have been at their zenith. The paints are gone at Buffalo Gap and the baton at Mound Bottom has to be "chalked" to really determine its detail. We're still the better however for having these examples at all. Someday nature will reclaim to the original condition through the processes of erosion and weathering the rocks that these pieces of art are painted on. That will be a sad day indeed. Let us be glad that in this small way we have been able to share in prehistoric man's thoughts and feelings across the centuries.

At Paint Rock Bluff the Harpeth enters Dickson County and from this point throughout the rest of its northward journey it serves as the

32. Stringfellow Bridge

dividing line between Dickson and Cheatham Counties. Swinging out of
Corlew's Bend the Stringfellow Bridge—-a huge, rusty, antiquated iron
bridge—is passed under, and a short time later the Ashland City Road is
left behind. Continuing on into Collier Bend the Harpeth receives the
waters of Jones Creek. It was on Jones Creek that Montgomery Bell had
three additional iron works: Upper Forge, Bellevue Forge, and Valley
Forge. This area lies in the same one-time rich iron belt of Western
Middle Tennessee. Town Creek, a small tributary to Jones Creek, runs
by Charlotte, the county seat of Dickson County. Charlotte received its
name from the wife of Nashville's founder and Cumberland Forge's first
owner, James Robertson.

Just about five miles further downstream the Harpeth deposits its
collections of hundreds of miles of tributaries into the Cumberland
River at what is known as Harpeth Shoals. The Cumberland here is part
of Cheatham Lake. Here, at the mouth of the Harpeth, over two hundred
years ago a band of Shawnee Indians was massacred by a party of
Cherokees and Chickasaws. The Shawnees had overstayed their welcome in this part of the country, having dwelt in a small town on the
site of North Nashville for some years before. Hostilities increased between them and the Cherokees, until the Shawnees decided to pull up
stakes ànd move on. They got no further than Harpeth Shoals by canoe
when a trap, set by the Cherokees and Chickasaws, caught them un-
aware. The entire party of Shawnees was annihilated.

Over the years the Harpeth and its tributary system has been very fortunate in not having had any of its length disturbed by power and flood control projects. At a time when dam building seems almost a craze in order to fulfill hydroelectric needs of a growing population, it is a wonder that the Harpeth has not been tapped. Maybe it does not offer the potentitalities that the Corps of Engineers looks for when scouting new territory for harnessing power. Whatever the reason, I hope this will always be the case.

One fancy project, which ended before it started good, was contemplated years ago for the Harpeth. The Harpeth Navigation Company was established in 1813 in order to provide steamboat communications between Franklin and Nashville. The company received authorization to sell stock and to construct dams and locks along the river in order to achieve a navigable stream to its mouth. The project was unsuccessful and never really got off the ground. As one witty sage remarked at the time, "The only difficulty, I think, is a lack of water."

And so the Harpeth exists today much as it always has. Of course all of the forests are gone, and poor farming methods all along its course have in the past caused and continue to cause untold thousands of tons of valuable top soil to be dumped into it. But aside from it not being as clear as it used to be, and aside from the face of the countryside around it having changed so drastically, it is still the same old Harpeth. And in an age when nothing much is the same as it used to be, this is good.

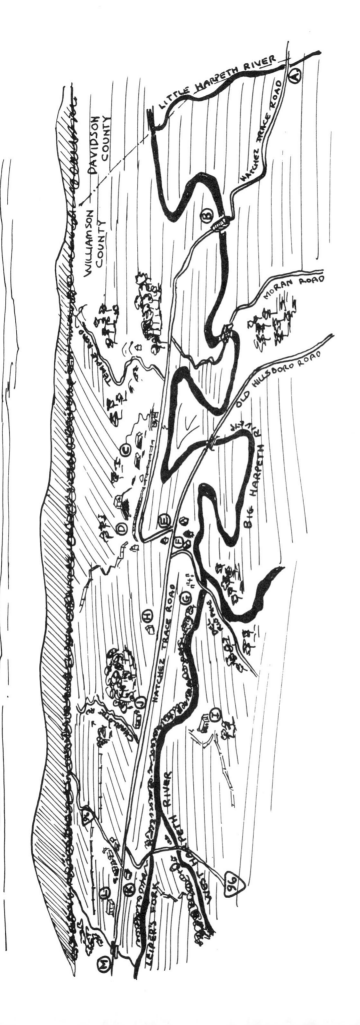

33 *Map of the Natchez Trace Road showing historic points of interest.*

A. Where the Natchez Trace Road crosses the Little Harpeth.
B. Union Bridge
C. Old Town
D. Montpier

E. Forest Home
F. Meeting of the Waters
G. The Perkins Cemetery
H. Site of Old Toll-House
I. Walnut Hill

J. Site of Hillside
K. Old Toll-House at Leiper's Fork
L. T. H. Benton's Boyhood Home
M. Site of Cunningham's Bridge

Chapter 8

The
Natchez Trace

From time immemorial the animal trail, later adopted by the Indians and known alternatively as the Natchez or Chickasaw Trace, has left what is known today as Nashville and headed off in a southwestwardly direction toward the Lower Mississippi country. The Trace, which passed through Nashville and became part of a larger trail system in the Southeast, provided transportation for herds of buffalo and possibly other game, as well as for the Indians in their wanderings from village to village. The present location of Nashville contained a huge salt lick known to the early settlers as the French Lick, and it was this place that held an attraction for the large animal herds, particularly the buffalo. These concentrations of large numbers of animals in one place in turn attracted Indians who could, in a short time among such concentrations, acquire quite a supply of fresh meat for their needs.

Leaving Nashville the Natchez or Chickasaw Trace headed off in a westwardly direction more or less along the path of West End Avenue. It passed Cockrill Springs which was located just off of West End in present day Centennial Park. It then continued its generally westward journey past Dunham's Spring on the future Belle Meade mansion grounds, across Richland Creek and on out to the vicinity of Bellevue; thence it ran to Pasquo, or as it was called in the early days, Tank. From Pasquo the Trace climbed Backbone Ridge and headed generally southwestward into the Duck River watershed area. From this point it continued toward the southwest until it ended in the vicinity of present day Natchez, Mississippi.

The Natchez Trace *Road* or the "Government" Road as it is some-

34. Union Bridge

times called is an altogether different thoroughfare than the Natchez *Trace*. The Natchez Road really has no relationship with the Natchez Trace except that they do converge and become one a few miles south of Nashville. The Government Road was built in 1801-02 by the United States Army as a response to legislation passed by Congress in 1800 establishing a post road between Nashville and Natchez. The existing route, that is the primitive Trace, was not satisfactory for the mail service to operate on, hence the Government's involvement in improving this thoroughfare. A treaty on October 24, 1801, with the Chickasaw Indians and one a few weeks later with the Choctaws made the improvements upon the road possible.

When the people of the young town of Franklin, Tennessee heard of the Army's plans to build a road from Nashville generally southward, they urgently requested that it come through their town so that they

35. Old Store on Natchez Trace Road

would be on a direct mail hook-up. The Army refused, however, to honor this request and Franklin was completely by-passed by the road. This refusal to run the post road through Franklin made it necessary for the town to build its own road, later known as Carter's Creek Pike, to link up with the "Government" or Natchez Trace Road at the village of Hillsboro, now called Leiper's Fork.

The Government Road, completed in 1802, linked Nashville on the north with the original Trace on the south just after the Road crossed Cunningham's Bridge over Garrison Fork. At this point the Road travelled upward until it met the old Trace along the ridge line on Duck River Ridge, then travelled southwestwardly along the original part of the Trace. Let us now then explore the Government Road from its beginnings at Nashville to its terminus with the Old Trace beyond

Cunningham's Bridge, since this route lies for a large portion of its length in the valleys of the Little, Big and West Harpeth Rivers.

The Government Road had its northern terminus outside of Nashville in the vicinity of Old Hickory Boulevard. The present road leading south from the point near the present steeplechase grounds at Percy Warner Park has been called several names over the past few years, namely Stockitt Road, Vaughn's Gap Road, and Vaughn Road. Apparently it was changed from Vaughn's Gap Road to Vaughn Road in recent years in order to avoid confusion with the other Vaughn's Gap Road that lies to the west and north on the other side of Highway 100. It was originally called Stockitt Road after the Stockitt family that lived in this area and ran a mill for some years.

In any event, leaving what is now the area of Old Hickory Boulevard, the Trace Road took off in a southerly direction and pretty generally followed the present day Vaughn Road, across the Little Harpeth River at the Williamson County line, and on out to the junction formed by Vaughn and Sneed Roads. Sneed Road along this section, until relatively recent times, was called Union Bridge Road. The Road shifted directions at this junction and went generally westward for a few thousand feet, crossing the Big Harpeth in doing so. Union Bridge, which in later years carried the Trace Road across the Big Harpeth at this point, was built around 1881. It was a wooden covered bridge and one of the last of this type to survive in this part of the country. The bridge spanned the river about one hundred yards or so upstream from where the new bridge crosses it, and the original stone abuttments can still be seen along with part of the original roadbed as it leaves the bridge remains on the west bank of the river. Prior to the construction of Union Bridge, there was an earlier one at this place which was destroyed during the Civil War. Prior to this earlier version, travelers along the Trace Road had to utilize various fords in the area. After the Trace Road crossed the Harpeth, it continued in a westwardly direction for a hundred yards or so, and then turned south to follow the river along the road that presently bears the name, Old Natchez Trace.

On went the Trace Road, ever southward, past the place where present day Moran Road leads in from the east, on through the dense forest past the junction of it and present day Temple Road coming in from the west, on and on till it reached Brown's Creek. The road crossed Brown's Creek just as the creek enters the Big Harpeth from the west. Here, at this spot, one can still see the old stone bridge built by the

36. Stone Bridge at Old Town

Army during the 1801-1802 roadbuilding campaign. The roadbed leading up to the bridge from the north is still visible also. If one stands on the new bridge on the present road and looks at the old bridge, the old road can be seen on the right for quite a few feet.

The stone abutments to the old bridge are probably as strong today as they were when they were new. But the roadbed has suffered the wear and tear of decades of disuse and the elements. It is indeed in an ill state of repair at this time. It seems a shame that this bridge that has absorbed the footsteps of rich and of poor, of soldier and of outlaw, in war and in peace should come to such an inglorious ending as that which it will surely receive. Someday, not too far in the future and maybe before the reader sees these pages, this little monument to the imagination of a young nation and the engineering ability of the U. S. Army, will crumble to pieces. Having deposited its last remains into the little creek below, it will soon be forgotten just like the ancient village that used to be at Old Town.

Old Town, called such because of the ancient Indian habitation site which used to set on the property, has a double history. The ancient part, that of the early Indian habitation, will be discussed in depth in another chapter. The more recent history of Old Town needs examination at this point however.

The land which once contained the vast Indian village, and which now is part of what is known as Old Town, was part of property originally owned by John Donelson, who came to Nashboro from the Wautauga settlements aboard the "Adventure". Since Tennessee at that time was not a state yet, this land was granted to Donelson by the State of North Carolina. Donelson left the property to his son John Donelson, Jr., who later sold it to William O'Neal Perkins. Perkins was a son of Nicholas Perkins, builder of Montpier which lies along the Trace Road a little further south. Thomas Brown bought the land from Perkins on July 13, 1840 and his residence, which today is the home of Mr. and Mrs. Henry Goodpasture, was completed in 1846. The little creek which flows through the property and which was crossed by the old bridge mentioned above was originally called Donelson's Creek, after John Donelson. In later years it was changed to Brown's Creek to reflect the new owner. This stream is still called Brown's Creek to this day according to current maps of the area.

Mr. Brown was originally from Virginia, as were so many early residents of this area. The beautiful house that Brown built was two-storied and was made out of hand-hewn timbers. Mr. Brown's sons served proudly in the Confederate Army and tradition has it that Grandma Brown stood on the balcony of the fine home at Old Town and watched the wounded soldiers pass by on the Trace Road as they retreated from the Battle of Franklin.

A little further down Natchez Trace Road lies Montpier, the home place of Nicholas Perkins. Perkins was a noted lawyer in Franklin and served in the Tennessee Senate for one term in 1815-17. Perkins was born in Pittsylvania County, Virginia, in 1779. He was a descendant of the first Nicholas Perkins who settled in tidewater Virginia in 1641. The younger Nicholas moved from his home to Washington County in the Mississippi Territory in 1801. In order not to be confused with others of the same name in that area, he was known locally as "Bigbee" Nicholas Perkins, because his home was on the Tombigbee River.

In February, 1807, while a resident of Washington County, Perkins captured Aaron Burr, former Vice-President of the United States, and returned with him to Richmond, Virginia, where Burr stood trial for treason. Chief Justice John Marshall heard the evidence in the case and in September, 1807, Burr was acquitted of the charge. Perkins left Richmond and went to Washington, and according to Jonathan Daniels in his fine book on the Natchez Trace, *The Devil's Backbone,* received President Jefferson's thanks and a reward of $3,331.

Perkins came to Williamson County from Washington and was married in 1808 to his cousin, Mary Harden Perkins, known as "Pretty Polly". He established his huge estate of 12,000 acres in 1810, which was at the time the largest tract of land in Williamson County owned by one individual. He completed his brick mansion just to the west of Natchez Trace in 1826. He died in 1848 and was known at his death as one of the largest landowners in the state. Nicholas Perkins is buried in the Perkins Cemetery just off Del Rio Pike, a little over a mile southeast of Montpier.

Nicholas and "Pretty Polly" had eleven children. One of their sons was William O'Neal Perkins, who was born in 1815. William O'Neal is the one who bought the property that Old Town is situated on from John Donelson, Jr. and from whom Thomas Brown bought it in 1840. Perkins in later life became President of the Tennessee and Alabama Railroad which was chartered in 1852 and was originally scheduled to run from Nashville to the Alabama line. The plans were later changed so that the line ended at Mt. Pleasant. This line later became an important part of the Louisville and Nashville Railroad. Another son of Nicholas and his wife was Nicholas Edwin Perkins, who was born in 1821 and died in 1871 at his homeplace, "Meeting of the Waters", situated on Del Rio Pike where the West Harpeth flows into the Big Harpeth.

From the vicinity of Montpier the Natchez Road continues its southerly journey until it comes to the west of the community of Forest Home. There, at the present day Church of Christ, the Trace originally continued in its general direction rather than following the abrupt curve that is present in the road today. Since it continued on in a more or less southerly direction, it by-passed the actual community of Forest Home and angled off to the southwest on the west side of the present Old Hillsboro Road at a point a few hundred feet beyond Forest Home. For the rest of the Trace's journey to Leiper's Fork it ran alongside, on the west, of present day Old Hillsboro Road.

It is apparent from the foregoing that the original Hillsboro Pike, known now as the Old Hillsboro Road, followed the original route of the Natchez Trace Road from a point just south of Forest Home all the way to Hillsboro, or as it is called today, Leiper's Fork. A direct quote from the original Government study of the Trace at the time the Parkway was proposed pretty well confirms this. Senate Document Number 148, *The Natchez Trace Parkway Survey,* states "from this property", (speaking of T. H. Benton's boyhood home to be discussed shortly) "it continued on through Leiper's Fork and along the general route of the highway to Forest Home."

Just about a mile beyond Forest Home on the present Old Hillsboro Road there stood a toll gate for the Hillsboro Turnpike as this successor to the Trace was later called. The toll gate is plotted on an 1878 map of Williamson County, yet Goodspeed's history indicates that the Hillsboro Turnpike was a free road to within one quarter mile of the village of Hillsboro, and that from there on out south to Cunningham's bridge it was owned by the South Harpeth Turnpike Company and that it had one toll gate. In any event, judging from the map's location of the toll gate south of Forest Home, it would be just about in the vicinity of where present day Barrel Springs Hollow Road meets Old Hillsboro Road from the west. Of course, there is no evidence of such a place now. Years of the plow and later road construction have obliterated any remains that might have shown where this gate stood.

Returning to the Natchez Trace Road and considering it synonymous now with the Old Hillsboro Road from the general vicinity of Forest Home, it goes on southwestwardly until it passes "Walnut Hill" on the east. "Walnut Hill" is one of the several homes that Nicholas Perkins built for his various children. Continuing onward, ever southwestward, the Trace passes the site where "Hillside" used to stand. "Hillside" was the homeplace of yet another Perkins, this one however from another branch of the family. Samuel F. Perkins, master of "Hillside", was born in Williamson County in 1833 and grew to be one of the county's most

37. "Hillside" Just Prior to Destruction

successful farmers. His farm consisted of 700 acres, and the house stood at the intersection of the Trace and the Charlotte Road. Perkins was in the Confederate Army during the Civil War and afterwards returned to "Hillside" to resume his farming endeavors. He died at his home in 1885.

"Hillside" stood for years after its last resident left, and through these years it suffered from time and the elements. It was a very becoming house even in its decline, and I have often driven by and looked upon it and wondered what wonderful tales it could tell. In later years the old house became a barn and contained hay for the cattle that grazed on what used to be its front lawn. Weeds, brush, and trees cluttered around what was left of the house. Finally, two or three years ago, "Hillside" burned. I very well remember the shock when I first learned that this old mansion was no longer there. After years of seeing it just setting there, it was quite a blow to discover that it was destroyed. "Hillside" now is nothing but a memory to those who were fortunate enough to remember it.

Today, just beyond the place where "Hillside" stood, new Highway 96 has been pushed through from Old Hillsboro Road to Highway 100. This section completes the linkup of Franklin with Linton. The route lies through some truly beautiful country, and the drive through can be made in 10 or 15 minutes. I wonder how many minutes it used to take by horseback or on foot to travel from Franklin to what is now Highway 100 by way of the Old Charlotte Road?

The Trace continues on its way beyond its intersection with Highway 96 until it comes to the Bingham Community. Passing through here it continues until it reaches Leiper's Fork, formerly known as Hillsboro. Just beyond the junction of the Trace and old Highway 96 coming in from Franklin to the east is an old toll building on the east side of the highway. This toll building was used for the Hillsboro Road of later times rather than the Natchez Trace. The old gate was closed for its last time sometime around 1927. It cost a dime to get through the gate in those days. It seems that this might be the gate referred to earlier in this chapter as the one being within one quarter of a mile of Hillsboro. The old building is in an ill state of repair and probably won't be standing much longer.

Continuing on the Trace passes through Leiper's Fork and about a mile or so beyond passes the site of Thomas Hart Benton's boyhood home. Benton's family came to this section of Williamson County in 1799 from North Carolina. They located on a grant of some 2,500 acres which lay just north of the Indian Boundary Line. Benton practiced law in Franklin and was quite well known there in his younger years. Benton's brother, Jesse, who also lived at the homeplace before going to Nashville to live, is best remembered in these parts for the gunshot wound he gave Andrew Jackson during a fracas between Jackson and the two brothers on the Nashville Square. Jackson suffered the effects of this wound for several years and friendship was never re-established between him and Jesse. Tom Benton, however, became reconciled with Jackson over the years, and the two became friends again.

Tom Benton was a State Senator from Williamson County during the 1809-11 term while he was practicing law in Franklin. In 1815 when he was 31 years old he moved to Missouri. He was destined for fame there also, and in 1821 he was elected to the United States Senate and served there for thirty years. Though Missouri claims Tom Benton as its own, and justifiably so, we Tennesseans can point with pride that the man's formative years were spent right here in Williamson County. The original Benton home burned in later years and nothing but the foundations remained. Another home was built upon these foundations later, and this is the house that can be seen today on the west side of the Trace Road.

38. Toll House at Leiper's Fork

39. Thomas Hart Benton's Boyhood Home

Beyond the Benton property the Trace Road continues until it comes to Cunningham's Bridge. This is the point where the Trace Road left the lowlands and climbed the Duck River Ridge to meet the original Natchez Trace on the crest of the ridge. The original Government study says,

> "At the point where the Trace begins to ascend the Duck River Ridge, it crosses Leiper's Fork of the West Harpeth River by means of the Cunningham Bridge, which is a very small structure. This point is notable because it marks the northern terminus of the ridge road and from it the Natchez Trace could have taken several routes into Nashville."

Actually, Cunningham's Bridge crosses Garrison Creek which is a tributary of Leiper's Fork. Garrison Creek received its name because a garrison of U.S. soldiers was stationed there in the early part of the nineteenth century. The route taken into Nashville from this point follows the Hillsboro Road to Forest Home and thence along the present day Old Natchez Trace to Sneed Road, thence to Vaughn Road and on to Old Hickory Boulevard; i.e., the route that we have been exploring in this chapter. This entire section was known as the "Government Road".

The original Trace, rather than dropping off at Cunningham's Bridge, continued on northward across Backbone Ridge and as previously stated came off of this ridge in the vicinity of present day Pasquo on Highway 100. The original Trace continues on in the other direction through the rest of Williamson County and throughout most of Maury County along the spine of Duck River Ridge. It leaves the Harpeth River Valley in these parts, therefore, this is as far as we will follow it in this narrative.

After several years of booming traffic, the Natchez Trace slowly began to play second place to river traffic and better highways that delivered their freight and passengers much faster than the older, more

40. The Site of Cunningham's Bridge

primitive Trace. In the years of its glory, however, it saw the passage of many famous personages. Andrew Jackson brought his wife, Rachel, back along the Trace in 1791, and it was during another northward journey along the Trace during the War of 1812 that Jackson received his nickname "Old Hickory" because of the tough measures he utilized in getting his Tennessee soldiers back from Mississippi after having been ordered to dismiss them with no pay. Thomas and Jesse Benton travelled it countless times, along with the Perkins' and Meriwether Lewis, recently back from the famous Lewis and Clark Expedition to the Pacific Ocean, met his fate on the Trace a little further to the south at Grinder's Stand.

So the Trace is a highway of history. From its beginnings as an animal trail connecting favorable feeding and watering places, to an Indian trail connecting villages, to a settlers' highway connecting two bustling frontier towns, the Trace has seen and heard its share of the history of our country. Today, final plans are being made for the completion of the northern section of the Natchez Trace Parkway on into Nashville. Rather than follow the Government Road from Cunningham's Bridge into Nashville to terminate at Old Hickory Boulevard and Percy Warner Park, it will follow the crest of Backbone Ridge until it drops down at Pasquo. Thus the Parkway, in its northern extremity, will follow the original Indian path preserving for those of us with an exploring spirit the opportunity to see the Trace the way it was before the first whites got into these parts.

Chapter 9

Good Guys and
Bad Guys

The Valley of the Harpeth has had its share of notable men, both
in a local and a national sense. We have already discussed Nicholas
Perkins who must have been one of the richest men in the area during
his lifetime. We have mentioned Thomas Hart Benton who became one
of the most important national figures of his time. There are many,
many more that could be mentioned who—because of their vast land-
holdings, or their influence in their respective communities, or their
impact on local and national politics—have earned their names a place
in the history of this area.

Probably one of the most famous people to emerge from the valley
was Matthew Fontaine Maury. His fame and works were not only na-
tionally famous; they were internationally famous. During his lifetime he
received awards and medals from the major powers of Europe reward-
ing him for the outstanding work that he did in the exploration of the
sea. Two of these countries, Russia and France, even extended an invi-
tation for him to live there. "Pathfinder of the Seas" was a just name
for this man who did so much to benefit today's maritime industry.

Maury was descended from a Huguenot family on his father's side.
His paternal grandfather was the Reverend James Maury, an Episcopal
minister and schoolteacher. Reverend Maury had the distinction of having taught three future Presidents of the United States, as well as five
future signers of the Declaration of Independence. Reverend Maury
possessed a certain amount of armchair wanderlust, and in his classes
he used to point to the map of the then unexplored western section of
our hemisphere and exclaim that if there was a river flowing out of the

mountains on their eastern slopes (the Missouri), there must be one opposite, flowing down the western slopes and entering the Pacific Ocean. His teachings found fertile ground, because years later they were remembered by one of his students, President Thomas Jefferson. Jefferson had always had a keen eye for exploration, probably dating back to his childhood years when he was under the guidance of Reverend Maury.

41. Matthew Fontaine Maury's Boyhood Home

To satisfy his urge to explore the western section of our country, he organized the Lewis and Clark expedition which reached the Pacific Coast in 1805, via the Missouri-Columbia River route.

Matthew was born in Spottsylvania County, Virginia, about ten miles from Fredericksburg on January 24, 1806. When he was four years old his family migrated to Williamson County, Tennessee, and settled on a farm northwest of Franklin. Matthew's uncle, Abram Maury, was already a resident in that area and this is probably why the family came. It will be recalled that Abram Maury owned the land upon which Franklin was founded. Maury County, upon its later formation, was named in Abram's honor.

When he was twelve years old, Matthew entered the Harpeth Academy. Having suffered an accident about that time in which he almost bit off his tongue and severely injured his back, his father thought it best to enter him in school since it appeared that he would be handicapped as far as farm work was concerned. In 1825 Congressman Sam Houston obtained a Midshipman's Warrant in the United States Navy for young Matthew. Matthew's father was adverse to his accepting this warrant since an elder son had already perished at sea. He never absolutely refused his son this opportunity, however, and Matthew accepted. His entire life from that point on was devoted to the Navy. In later life he turned his attention to the more scholarly aspects of his profession, and his later researches in oceanography and meteorology were eagerly accepted all over the world.

When, during the brooding period preceding the Civil War, it became obvious that the South would secede from the Union, Maury devoted his full energies to divert this course. When it was apparent, however, that nothing could be done about the national situation, he resigned his commission in the United States Navy and joined forces with the Confederacy. After the war Maury accepted an offer to teach physics at the Virginia Military Institute. He pursued these interests until his death in February of 1873. He was buried at the Lexington, Virginia, Cemetery, but was later removed to the Hollywood Cemetery on the James River.

No less famous in these early years of the valley's history was John Bell. Bell has been described as being one of the most prominent politicians in the United States during the years 1825 to 1860. He excelled in oratory no less than he did in his clear thinking on the political issues of the day. Born in Davidson County on Mill Creek in 1796, Bell was graduated from Cumberland College in 1814. He took up the practice of law in Williamson County in 1816. When he was only 21 years old, in 1817, he was elected to the Tennessee Senate, representing Williamson County. After this early step into politics, Bell realized that he needed more practical experience before he would be able to devote his full energies to the political scene. He therefore did not seek election to the State House again. In 1820 or 21 he moved to Murfreesboro and stayed there until he moved to Nashville in 1822. While in Nashville he lived in the residence at the corner of Spring and High Streets (Church at 6th Avenue).

As young Bell advanced in years and legal experience he began to delve into politics again. He was a Democratic-Republican by party, and in 1827 he ran for the United States Congress against Felix Grundy. While Bell was a friend of Andrew Jackson, Jackson did not hide the fact that he supported Grundy in the election. This caused a rift between Bell and Jackson that widened over the years and finally ended with Bell's renunciation of Jackson's politics and the Democratic-Republican Party.

Bell was victor of this election, however, in spite of Jackson's endorsement of Grundy. In his first term in Congress, Bell shared the Tennessee delegation with James K. Polk and David Crockett. He served a total of fourteen years in the House of Representatives, and it was during his seventh year in Washington City that he was elected Speaker of the House. The following year, 1835, saw the defeat of Bell in his bid for the Speaker's seat when James K. Polk won that position in the House's leadership.

In 1841 President Harrison appointed Bell to his Cabinet as Secretary of War. Harrison's early death, however, put Bell out of a job when Harrison's successor appointed a new Secretary. After this high point in his career, Bell retired from politics and re-entered private life. Getting back into politics in 1847, he was sent to the United States Senate. He had already renounced Democratic-Republicanism by this time and had joined forces with the Whig Party. He served in the Senate until 1859.

In 1860 another presidential election was coming up. The Democrats offered Stephen Douglas and the Republicans were represented by Abraham Lincoln. There were dissident groups in this country that could not lend their support to either of these candidates. One such group met in Baltimore in May of 1860 and formed the Constitutional Union Party. The nominees for this party were John Bell for President and Edward Everett for Vice-President. Bell's chief competition came from another Tennessean, Sam Houston. The new party, scornful of the platforms offered by the other two parties, ran on a ticket which merely supported the Union, the Constitution, and the enforcement of laws. The outcome of the election, of course, is well known. Abraham Lincoln won, but John Bell did carry the states of Tennessee, Virginia, and Kentucky. This lofty aspiration to political office was the last that John Bell was to take. He retired from politics after the election of 1860 and never sought public office again.

In the threatening days before the Civil War, Bell had steadfastly maintained his position for Union solidarity. He strongly disapproved of President Lincoln's handling of affairs after the war started, however, especially his call for the mustering of troops from Tennessee. The mental struggle that took place in Bell's mind at this time must have been intense. On the one side was his love for the Union while on the other was his love for the South and his disapproval of the way the war was being pursued by those in the North. So at last, he did like so many other great men of the South did in those trying times; he aligned himself with the Southern cause. While he did not actually engage in the war itself, he did wholeheartedly lend his support to the Confederacy.

Bell died in September of 1869 at the Cumberland Iron Works. With his passing a whole era of Tennessee politics, dominated by himself over many years, passed also. Indeed an era of national politics passed too, because in his time John Bell was probably the most intellectual, keen sighted politician in Washington.

For some reason throughout our Nation's history, the frontier areas have always produced a breed of men who adapted and who usually provided the leadership qualities which our young country so vitally needed in those days. The history of the expanding frontier is full of the names of Americans who achieved national fame through their exploits. Tennessee was no different. It gave the country its best in Andrew Jackson, James K. Polk, Sam Houston, and David Crockett, among others. The Harpeth Valley was no different either. Out of the raw towns and the rough farms of this five county area came many famous Americans from the days of the earliest settlement right on down to the 1970's. Maury and Bell were chosen from among the list, because they happened to reach just about the ultimate that their careers could offer.

Unfortunately, the frontier not only brings out the best qualities in some men; it also brings out the worst qualities in others. For every notable valley dweller there was probably a scoundrel, and some of these scoundrels, like some of their more legitimate neighbors, achieved a fair degree of success and fame. The success was shortlived for most, however, even though the fame lived on.

It should be no surprise that the Harpeth River Valley and the surrounding territory during the last years of the eighteenth century and the early years of the nineteenth was a hangout for the lawless and rough and ready element that has gone hand in hand throughout our history with the advancement of the frontier. The proximity of the

Natchez Trace, along with the fact that during these years this section was the leading edge of pioneer exploration and settlement in this part of the expanding United States, makes it easier to understand why this area may have had a little more than its share of lawlessness.

The reader is already familiar with the Harpe Brothers from an earlier reference to them. These fellows formed the vanguard of a long line of criminal elements that was to parade through the old Southwest for many years to follow. I have already spoken of the perfect environment for this criminal element that the Natchez Trace afforded with its north-bound traffic of monied travelers. This extra attraction of a concentration in one general area of so many possible victims, coupled to the wild environs that the slowly expanding frontier afforded, made the section under discussion the northern terminus for much devilment during these early years.

One of the most interesting early court cases in the town of Franklin was decided on April 14, 1823. In the case John A. Murrell was found guilty and fined fifty dollars for "riot". His brother, William, and he were also bound over in the amount of two-hundred dollars to "keep the peace". John Murrell was only in his late teens at that time, but three years before he had already started his long career as one of the most notorious highwaymen in the old Southwest.

Murrell was born around Columbia, Tennessee in 1804. His criminal activities began at the age of sixteen, when he robbed his mother's money box along with a pistol and some other items from one of his mother's suitors. His flight from this crime launched him on a career that was to span a decade and a half, and into one which would bring terror into every community in the South. Murrell participated in crimes ranging from robbery to murder; from horse theivery to slave stealing. His biggest effort, though one which fortunately never occurred, was his plot to foment a slave revolt which would take place simultaneously all over the South. This revolt, which was nursed over several years in the minds of Murrell and his associates, was to take place on Christmas Day, 1835. This fantastic scheme was the product of Murrell's wild imagination while he was serving in prison for one year at the State Penitentiary in Nashville for horse stealing. For this crime, he also received 39 lashes upon his back at the Nashville Courthouse and had the letters H. T.—which stood for Horse Thief—branded into his left thumb.

In order to finance his slave rebellion, Murrell took up slave stealing after his release from the penitentiary. His gang would proposition a slave into being "stolen" under the pretense that they would get the slave's freedom by channeling him to the North by way of the Under-

42. Murrel Stealing a Slave

ground Railroad which was already active by that time. They would then resell the slave, explaining to him that this was necessary to help defray the expenses. At this point they would steal the slave again, this time from his new owner. Then the whole cycle would repeat itself with the slave always expecting that the next move would be the one in which he gained his freedom. This last act, of course, never was realized.

Murrell's organization which would fan the fires and spread the flames of the proposed slave rebellion was called the Mystic Clan. The Clan was later organized into various levels of authority and adopted a code system, an identification sign, and other clannish type rituals. Through the efforts of an inside spy, Murrell was finally caught and jailed before the uprising could take place. He was tried in Jackson, Tennessee. For some reason he was only charged with, and found guilty of, slave stealing. He received a ten-year prison sentence to be served in the State Penitentiary at Nashville.

After Murrell's confinement to prison, his Mystic Clan organization slowly began to fall apart. There was no one in it with the drive or the organizing genius that Murrell had provided before his confinement.

Therefore, when December 25, 1835—the proposed date for the slaves' uprising—arrived, it was no different than any other day. Murrell lived to see the outside world again, but when he left prison he was a diseased and broken man. He took a job as blacksmith in the vicinity of Pikeville, Tennessee, but survived for only a short time after his release from prison. He supposedly is buried in a church cemetery somewhere in Bledsoe County.

Thus ended the career of one of the most notorious outlaws the United States had ever known up to that time, or has ever known since. When Murrell's crimes are compared to those of later, more famous outlaws of the western section of our country, these later criminals appear mild indeed. From a simple beginning with his day in court in Franklin, John A. Murrell surely went a long way. Had his genius been channelled in the right direction, we might be reading of him and his endeavors with admiration rather than among the ranks of outlawry.

Chapter 10

The
Old Ones

As we walk or drive through the beautiful Harpeth River Valley today with its fine herds of cattle, its tall green corn, and its lovely horses,
we would hardly suspect that a short six to seven hundred years ago this
same area was a bustling center for thousands of Indians of the Temple
Building Cult, known more scientifically as the Mississippian Period.
The temple mounds of these people are scattered all about a major
portion of Williamson and Cheatham Counties and in the surrounding
areas of Davidson County as well.

No less than five major population centers, three of them discussed
in this book, have been identified along the valley of the Harpeth River
and its tributaries. The traces of most of these sites can still be seen
rising out of the pastures and fields. Horses and cattle graze now on
what were once the religious centers of a vibrant, alert people. Trees
grow on top of mounds once used to support the houses of the chiefs
and the temples in which these people worshipped. Two hundred growing seasons have seen the plow go deeply into the plazas where people
by the hundreds once came to watch religious ceremonies long since
forgotten.

All these people were gone when the first settlers reached this part
of the country. The few Indians living here and there when these pioneers
came had long forgotten anything about the mounds and plazas that were
scattered over the countryside. By then trees of considerable size must
have covered all these sites since they had been in disuse for several
hundred years. We can imagine the surprise of an early settler coming
upon these ruins with their magnificent mounds, as he cleared the

forests for agricultural purposes. Some of the sites are gone forever, destroyed by the farmers plow. Some, however, have retained a semblance of their original shapes. Others are pretty well as they were hundreds of years ago, except for the houses and temples themselves, which of course are gone.

Before we survey the Harpeth River sites, it might be best to review briefly the origins of the American Indian so that we can gain a degree of insight into the background of the Temple Mound Builders and also the people who preceeded them. For certainly they were not the first prehistoric peoples of this area, but were rather near the last of a long line of several distinct populations to come and go in the Harpeth Valley. With this, albeit slight, background into the indigenous inhabitants of our area, we will be better prepared for a study of the Mississippian peoples who built the imposing temple mounds and other works which are the subject of the following chapters.

Nobody nowadays much argues with the fact that the countless migrations of herd-chasing hunters of Mongolian racial stock were responsible for the people we know today as American Indians. These Mongolians crossed the Bering Land Bridge during the last glaciation when Alaska and Siberia were joined by dry land. As these people chased the herds of animals that they depended on for food, clothing, and shelter, they had no way of knowing that they had crossed from one continent to another. These migrations could have started as long ago as 30-40 thousand years before the present, and very probably lasted up till only two thousand or so years ago when the ancestors of the Eskimos made their entrance upon the American scene. In any event these hunters gradually worked their way south until they had populated the entire Western Hemisphere from the Arctic tundra to the frozen wastes of Patagonia, thousands of miles to the south.

It is pretty well believed now that there have been random contacts between American Indians and other Asiatic people, notably the Japanese, through trans-Pacific voyages. Recent excavations in Ecuador would lead scientists to believe that an entire pottery style was quite possibly imported from Japan in its fully developed style, with no evolu-

43. A Clovis Point

tion of this style distinguishable in this hemisphere. There is also excellent documentation that there may have been European contacts with American Indians years before Columbus or the Norsemen. Whether or not this will ever be admitted by the scientific world remains to be seen. However, it is not the purpose at this time to debate pro or con in these arguments. The point is that the *origin* of American Indians, regardless of later possible contact with other populations, was Asiatic, and that these Asiatic peoples first saw the New World thousands of years ago when the migrations of these faceless wanderers carried them beyond the point of no return.

These new people maintained a hunting culture for untold hundreds and thousands of years. Archaeological evidence of this phase of their habitation has been found in Tennessee. This phase, known as the Paleo Culture expressed itself in the well known Clovis and Folsom fluted points. Clovis points have been found in various parts of Tennessee including all five counties that the Harpeth River flows through.

In Tennessee, after the Paleo stage of culture passed, came the Archaic. Archaic Culture saw an end to the endless wanderings of the hunting folk. Instead of groups on the move chasing the wild animal herds we find the beginning of settled life, even though the villages at that time were still small. The beginnings of agriculture are also apparent during the Archaic period. In addition to the game still brought home from the forest, the people of these times supplemented their diet with fish.

The next main period of culture was the Woodland Phase. The people of this culture period maintained the village life begun by the Archaic peoples. Agriculture became more and more important in the daily lives of these folks. The bow and arrow was introduced during these times and probably gradually replaced the spear as a weapon for both hunting and defense. Pottery came in vogue during the Woodland Period, attesting to a more and more settled life for these people. It was the people of the Woodland Culture who developed the concept of burying their dead in burial mounds. This culture was very widespread over the entire eastern United States, and most likely the influence for this sudden burst of mound building activity come from the southwest, possibly Central America and thereabout.

Finally we come to the Mississippian Culture. Most of the sites we will survey later in this book were built and inhabited during this culture phase. It is possible that when De Soto came through the Southeast that the Mississippian Culture was in its waning days. But no English-speaking pioneer ever saw evidence of this stage even in its twilight time,

44. A Temple Mound Village

because by the time that our ancestors started arriving in this part of the country the so-called Recent or Historical Period had already begun. The Mississippian Period is best remembered for the construction of the large, and in some cases still visible, temple mounds. Called temple mounds because of the practice of the mounds serving as a pedestal for the religious temples, this cultural idea is also believed to have been borrowed from south of the border, again probably from people in Central America.

In the Harpeth River area, as in other places, there was a gradual evolution of one cultural phase into another so that the inhabitants of the last phase didn't necessarily migrate anywhere or become extinct. They simply became blended in with new cultural ideas which were brought in by each new migration of peoples. Thus, over the years the Paleo people gradually evolved into the Archaic people, the stimulus for this evolution probably being a new migration from Asia. Likewise, the Archaic Culture blended into the Woodland, under the same conditions as above. Southwestern influences reached the Woodland people, thus starting them on their mound building activities. Finally, additional southwestern influences helped in the evolution of the Woodland people into the Mississippian.

This concept of evolution of culture explains the gradual shift of the emphasis of hunting to an increased interest in the settled way of life and agriculture. A hunter, always on the move following the great animal herds, has very little time for sedentary living. It is only with the advent of agriculture and an assured food supply does any population finally find one place to call home and settle down. We have seen that beginnings of agriculture were apparent in the remains of the Archaic Culture. This dependence upon crop raising grew and grew among certain Indian populations in this country until at last, in some of them, their entire livelihood was centered around agriculture.

45. Indian Maize Compared to Modern Corn

The agricultural idea is another influence that came from the southwest. Corn, it is now believed, originated in Central America millenia ago and became a commodity over the years with several Indian groups in the United States by gradual dissemination of the agricultural idea and the corn seed. By the time the Mississippian Culture Period arrived, the Middle Tennessee Indians had been raising corn and other staple crops for hundreds of years.

With this brief background of Indian origins and the evolution of Indian culture in Tennessee, we can now look at the Harpeth River Valley sites with a little more insight and depth.

46. Temple Mounds at Old Town

Chapter 11

Old Town

It's a little difficult to stand on the bridge over Brown's Creek on the Old Natchez Trace and realize that just beyond Henry Goodpasture's rail fence there once lived hundreds of people carrying out their everyday lives, and that the remains of this vast community constituted one of the most celebrated archeological finds in this part of the country. For this site is Old Town, excavated by Dr. Joseph Jones in 1868-69.

Old Town is different now and all but traces of the ancient habitation are gone. The two temple mounds are still visible in the side pasture facing the road between the creek and the river. They can be distinguished as small rises out of the grass. Buttercups line the fence now in the springtime, and in the summer the shade is so thick at the bridge that it looks as if the sun were behind a cloud. The bridge crosses Brown's Creek, or as it used to be known, Donelson's Creek, just before the creek runs into the Big Harpeth River. We know from maps that this creek formed one edge of the original fortifications of the pre-historic town that would come to be known as Old Town.

One of the burial mounds at Old Town is still slightly visible if one knows exactly where to look. It is scarcely a rise out of the grass now on the left of the driveway leading up to Mr. Goodpasture's beautiful home. But the fortifications and campsites and the plazas and the box burials are all gone, victim to time and change upon the land demanded by a growing population and land-hungry settlers.

So much for the present. When Jones excavated at Old Town in 1868-69, the fortified enclosure consisted of some 12 acres with a line of earthworks extending in cresent fashion for some 2,470 feet. The Big Harpeth River served as the other side of this defensive plan. By the time Jones excavated, the enclosure was already badly worn, but he estimated that originally the earthworks surrounding the enclosure were so steep that a horse could not be ridden over them.

In addition to the two temple mounds and the burial mound referred to above, there apparently was one more large burial mound upon which the residence now sets. At least 50 stone-lined graves were opened at the time of excavation, these being mainly on the river embankment in front of the residence and on the side of the earthworks next to the creek. The large temple mounds were about 112 feet by 65 feet and 11 feet high and 70 feet by 60 feet and 9 feet high. The small burial mound was 30 feet by 30 feet and 2.5 feet high. The two temple mounds were pyramidal in shape while the burial mounds were more or less round. Quite a few artifacts were taken from this site, among them earthenware vases, pots, much skeletal material, a pipe, various celts, and arrow and spear heads. One earthenware pot found on the site has four legs and looks remarkably similar to the old cast iron pots used by our own, not too distant ancestors.

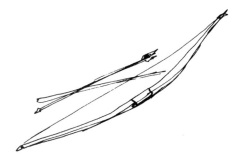

Go out to Old Town some day soon and stand there and gaze across Henry Goodpasture's rail fence at the remains of the two pyramidal temple mounds. Imagine the fence gone, and also the horses as they quietly graze, not knowing that the mouthful of grass that they chomp had roots in the very core of our country's history. Imagine, if you can, what this plot of land looked like six or seven hundred years ago when Mr. Goodpasture's house wasn't there, nor his barn, nor the paved road, nor the bridges.

If your imagination is vivid enough you will see a broad plaza reaching several hundred yards back from where you stand and extending about the same distance on either side. The beautiful hills still form the background in the west then as they do now. There is a steep drop behind you down to the river and you must be careful lest you trip backward and fall. Directly in front of you are the two temple mounds, each topped by a chief's dwelling or possibly a temple of some kind. These mounds are something to behold. They are much taller than they will be later when Jones describes them, and they both have thousands of cubic feet of earth and debris in them. How many bronze backs bent to the toil of carrying this load and for how long they stayed bent will never be known.

Let's leave our vantage point now and walk around the temple mounds toward the back perimeter of the fortifications. To our right is the creek with its steep embankments. As we follow the fortifications from the creek around the back side we marvel at the fine wooden stockade that crowns the earthworks all along the perimeter. It is pretty apparent that the folks we are visiting are well prepared against any outside attack from the pains they have taken to fortify their site. The way in which Old Town was fortified will cause Joseph Jones someday to write, "Old Town was admirably located for defense, and for an abundant supply of water and fish. On one side it was protected by the steep, abrupt banks of the Harpeth, and on the other, by a deep ravine and stream; whilst the remaining portions were protected by a high embankment, which was most probably crowned by a stockade during the occupation of the Aborigines."

As we pass an opening in the stockade on the back side of the enclosure we can peek through and see the corn and bean fields beyond. Here the women and children go out every day to work and care for the crops. It has been a good year and the crops are about ready for harvesting. With the beans, squash, and corn from the fields, supplemented by mussels from the river and wild game from the forests, it will truly be a good winter for our friends at Old Town.

As we walk back through the plaza to our original vantage point we

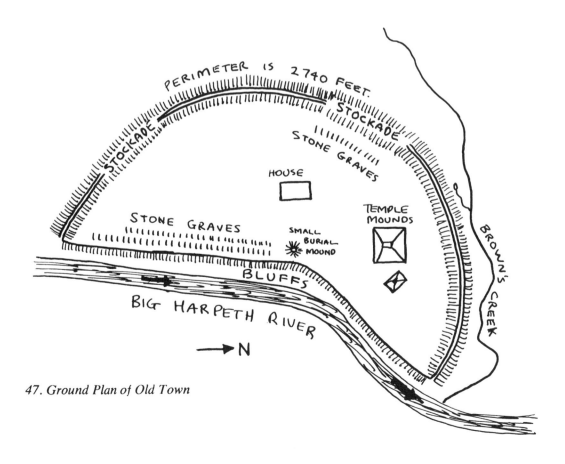

47. Ground Plan of Old Town

pass many individual houses scattered here and there across the broad expanse around the mounds. Cooking fires send smoke spiraling upward and the whole valley has a low cover of haze as the fragrant smell of the cooking fires permeates the entire village.

Regretfully now, we must return to the present. We have no way of knowing as we come back by the great temple mounds on our way out of the fortified village that in another hundred or so years our friends

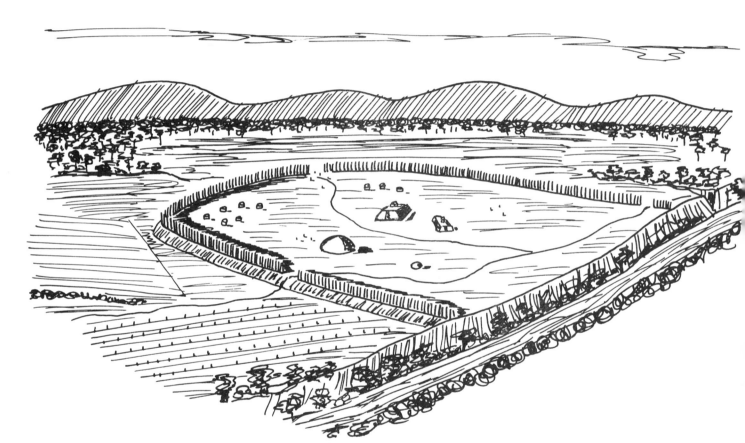

48. Old Town Village at its Zenith

at Old Town will have disappeared from the village that they fashioned so magnificently on the banks of the Big Harpeth. Dr. Jones someday will write that this curious, almost abrupt, disappearance could be credited to three reasons: "1. Emigration, 2. Destruction of the entire population by more barbarous and nomadic tribes, 3. Destruction by pestilence." In another passage Dr. Jones says, "It is evident from the age of the trees growing in many of these mounds," (here he was speaking of the ancient remains of Tennessee and other states generally, but

certainly Old Town qualified in this statement) "that they were completed and abandoned long before the discovery and exploration of the
North American Continent." In yet another passage, Dr. Jones states,

> "The numerous stone graves scattered over a belt of country
> stretching from the shores of Lake Erie to the borders of the pres-
> ent state of Georgia, are sad but unimpeachable witnesses of the
> fact that the fertile valleys of Ohio, Kentucky, and Tennessee were
> once filled with a numerous population; and the earthworks by
> which the mounds and graves are surrounded, bear testimony to
> the fierce and continued struggles in which these people were
> engaged with the more barbarous tribes; and the question arises,
> as we view these extensive graveyards, by what pestilence or
> calamity were they peopled?"

As explained in an earlier chapter, we know now that populations
do not necessarily have to be defeated and destroyed by a more power-
ful foe, nor do they simply disappear when their time is up. Rather we
know now, that instead of one of these alternatives, that one population
most likely blends in with a new influx of people so that gradually the
old concepts and ideas are replaced by the new until at last it appears
that no more of the old is left. This sort of acculturation most likely explains the disappearance of the inhabitants of Old Town and of all the
other sites that we will discuss in this book. Dr. Jones is possibly correct
in that one or all of his above reasons may have figured into the decline
of the Temple Building Cult in this part of the country. On the other
hand, the blending of the Temple Mound peoples with and into the
culture of other, newer arrived populations, probably best explains their
seemingly complete demise.

In any event the people of Old Town would gradually vanish, if not
from existence, at least from their village on the Harpeth. Fields would
lay deserted, grass would creep into the sacred plaza, and before too
many years the entire town would be grown over with brush and
weeds. With no one to maintain the mounds, they would gradually
begin to wash and erode to the extent that later, when the first white
settlers come into this country, they would be much smaller than they
once were. The posts making up the stockade would gradually begin to
lean to one side, and as year after year of rain and the elements do their
part in rotting the posts and with no one there to replace them with new
ones, this part of the fortification too would soon go back to dust. The
hardwood forest would close in inch by inch so that by the time Old
Town is looked on by white eyes, it is nothing more than a section of
forest containing gigantic trees, hundreds of years old. So, here is the
final phase of a story that goes back to the time the Crusaders were in

49. Earthenware Vessel from Old Town

the Holy Land trying to wrest the Holy Sepulcher from the Moslems. Perhaps the greatest indignity of the whole tale is that even the Indians that were here to meet the first whites had all forgotten about Old Town and couldn't remember what the mounds were or where they came from.

Chapter 12

The Fewkes Site

Out in Williamson County near the headwaters of the Little Harpeth lies the Fewkes Site. It lies on the right of Moore's Lane as one goes toward the Wilson Pike. The property is currently owned by the T. P. Primm, Sr. family who lives on Moore's Lane.

Excavated in October, 1920, by William Edward Myer of the Bureau of American Ethnology, the site was named in honor of Dr. J. Walter Fewkes who was at that time Chief of the Bureau. Dr. Jones made mention of this site as early as 1876 in his book, *Explorations of the Aboriginal Remains of Tennessee.* It was known in those days as Boiling Springs, apparently because of the springs that flow to the west of the site and which feed a small stream that runs into the Little Harpeth below the mounds area.

The main area of the Fewkes Site consisted of five mounds, the four largest forming somewhat of a square, and the fifth one lying off to the side on the small bluff which overlooks the Little Harpeth. The mounds area itself laid in the peninsula formed by the aforementioned spring-fed stream and the Little Harpeth River. The entire site consisted of some 14.6 acres. The site was fairly well excavated by Myer with the exception that Mound Number One was never dug into. Many burials were located and excavated and a variety of pottery remains, implements, stone idols, and other artifacts were found. The mounds themselves were just as impressive as the artifacts that were located thereabouts. Mound Number One reached a respectable height of 23 feet 8 inches and was 179 feet long by 166 feet wide. This was the highest mound and the one that is still visible today from the road. Looking from the fence which runs alongside Moore's Lane, Mound One lies just to the side of

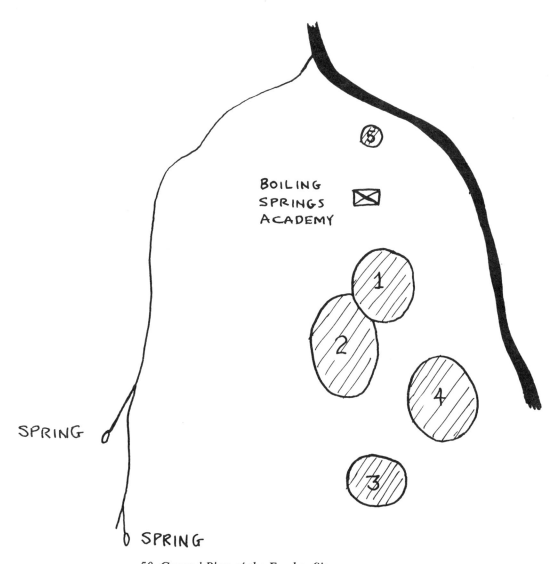

BOILING
SPRINGS
ACADEMY

SPRING

SPRING

50. Ground Plan of the Fewkes Site

the brick building that occupies the land between the mound and the river. While higher than the surrounding mounds, Number One was by no means the largest in area. Number Two, while not but 5 feet 7 inches high, measured an impressive 240 feet by 162 feet. Number Four was only 3 feet 8 inches high but measured 200 feet in length by 180 feet in width. Of course we can assume, I think, that time and the elements have worn a few feet off the height of all of these mounds so that in their prime, they were considerably more impressive than the current figures would indicate.

Mr. Myer expressed concern in his official report regarding this site,

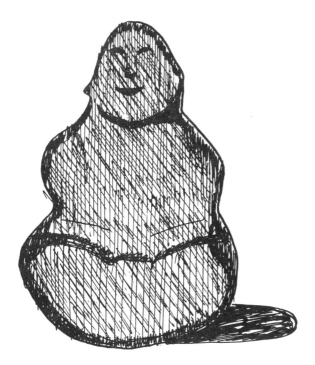

51. Stone Idol from the Fewkes Site

that during the entire excavation of the Fewkes Site and apparently several other Middle Tennessee sites as well, that no buffalo remains were found in the trash heaps or anywhere else within the village area for that matter. He made note of the fact that the early pioneers in the area al-

52. Vase from the Fewkes Site

53. Mound One of the Fewkes Site

ways commented upon the numerous herds of buffalo, and we all know
that most of our major highways leading in and out of Middle Tennessee
were originally buffalo trails, later adopted and shared by the Indians.
One of the possible reasons for this phenomenon could be, as Myer
explained, that the Indians did a full butchering job on the animals at
the kill site, and that they only brought back to camp those parts that
were edible. Still, it seems strange that no bony parts of the animal would
be found in view of the almost total use that the Plains Indians of historic times made of them.

This site probably dates back to the Mississippian period of habitation in Middle Tennessee as do the other sites discussed in this book.
For a minimum age we do have the fact that Myer had excavated at another site the month before he came to Fewkes, this first excavation
being in Davidson County and called Gordon's. The two sites were
probably inhabited at the same time and Myer found trees over 300
years old growing out of the tops of the ruins at the Gordon Site. He

also found a layer of 16 inches of black loam earth covering the floor of this site. Both of these examples testify to a very ancient age for Gordons and also Fewkes. How long it takes for nature to lay down a layer of soil 16 inches deep is anybody's guess, but I believe that a minimum of several hundred years would probably be required.

All that remains of the Fewkes Site now is Mound One. Undisturbed over the years it still pokes its top above the surrounding country side. Heavily covered with brush, its only visitors are a herd of cattle that graze this area frequently. With the construction of the new golf course next door, the future of the remains of the Fewkes Site seems dubious. We can only hope that somehow in this age of "progress" that modern man thinks enough of his heritage to allow this survival from the past to continue to exist as it has for so many hundreds of years.

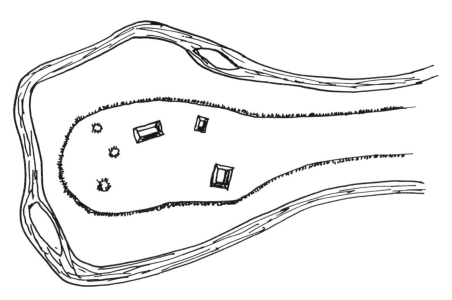

54. Ground Plan of Mound Bottom Division—Mound Bottom

Chapter 13

Mound
Bottom

Without question the Mound Bottom habitation site is the largest and most complex of all the prehistoric sites along the Harpeth River. Indeed, it is one of the largest in the entire southeastern United States. Mound Bottom is located in Cheatham County and parts of the site lie on both sides of U. S. Highway 70 just after it crosses the Harpeth River, about four miles west of the Davidson-Cheatham County line.

One of the earliest references to Mound Bottom is found in *Explorations of the Aboriginal Remains of Tennessee*. Dr. Jones very ably describes the extent of the place when he tells us:

> "Extensive fortifications several miles in extent, enclosing two systems of mounds, and numerous stone graves, lie along the Big Harpeth River about sixteen miles below Old Town, at Mound Bottom, and on Osborn's Place. Within these extraordinary aboriginal works which enclose the sites of two ancient cities, are found three pyramidal mounds about fifty feet in elevation and each one exposing about one acre of summit; and, besides these, are numerous lesser mounds."

Jones' reference to the remains at Osborn's Place refers to that area on the south side of Highway 70, while Mound Bottom proper lies on the north side. The two distinct areas of the site lie about a mile or so apart, and taken together cover some 500 acres.

William Edward Myer, who will be remembered from his work at the Fewkes Site, surveyed Mound Bottom for the Bureau of American Ethnology in 1923. He divided the area into the two parts referred to above, calling the one south of Highway 70 the "Great Mound" division and the one to the north the "Mound Bottom" division. Myer's exploration of the Great Mound Division indicated that the ancient inhabitants of this town had artificially leveled a natural hilltop until it was flat across the top. This broad plaza, which measured about 500 by 1000 feet, served in its northeastern quadrant as a base for the Great Mound. This mound can still be seen today from Highway 70.

Like other sites we have surveyed, the Great Mound Division was admirably situated for defense. The Harpeth River with its steep bluffs offered protection along the entire southern and eastern aspects of the town. Along the western and northern sides, an earthen embankment topped by a wooden stockade provided protection from these directions. Every few yards along the stockade there was a watch tower. The stockade itself showed evidence of having been plastered on the outer sides, making it more difficult for an attacker to climb. The watch towers projected beyond the walls, thereby providing the defenders with a certain degree of "cross-fire" ability. Myer found traces of some of the wood used in the construction of these towers and the stockade.

In addition to the Great Mound and its plaza, there were several other plazas and mounds within the Great Mound Division. Myer speculated that perhaps the inhabitants of this great town had at one time been divided into separate distinct groups, and that when all of them became grouped together at this site that they retained a semblance of their autonomy by having their own individual plaza areas with their associated mounds.

Myer was particularly impressed by the planning and beauty of this site. In the official report of his work, published in 1924, it was stated:

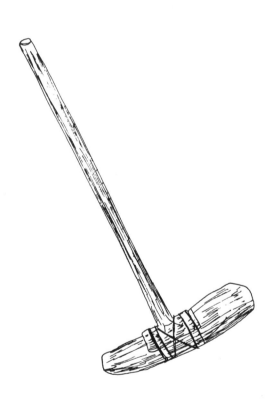

> "This prehistoric town is notable for the artistic ability displayed by the ancient man who planned the beautiful, terraced bold central hill with its fine plaza surmounted by towering Great Mound. No other remains of ancient man have been found in our southeastern United States which approach this Great Mound group in an artistic sense."

No one knows how many people lived in this section of the town. Surely, from the great effort obviously required to build the Great Mound and plazas and from the great pains these people went to in order to fortify their town, there must have been several thousand. Where did they go? No one knows. Myer did find evidence of fire in this part of the complex. Perhaps, on one bright day when everyone was going about his daily chores completely unsuspecting any danger, an enemy force did strike successfully. Scaling the walls on one side and the river bluffs on the other, these attackers fell upon the village killing, looting, and burning. After the battle, the village lay uninhabited. Gradually, the forest reclaimed the land, and the Great Mound Division was seen no more until the appearance of the first white settlers.

The other half of this vast complex, the Mound Bottom Division, lies a little over a mile off Highway 70 to the north on the road leading to the Narrows of the Harpeth. It takes up the entire bend of the Harpeth known locally as Mound Bottom. This division was originally connected with the Great Mound Division by a trail which in Jones' day was still visible as a well-worn path a foot lower than the surrounding area. This path, of course, is no longer visible today since all of the intervening land has been under the plow for generations.

Early white people in the area found a line of fortifications with towers alongside the river at this site. No evidence of these walls or towers was found by Myer. This division was as well-situated for

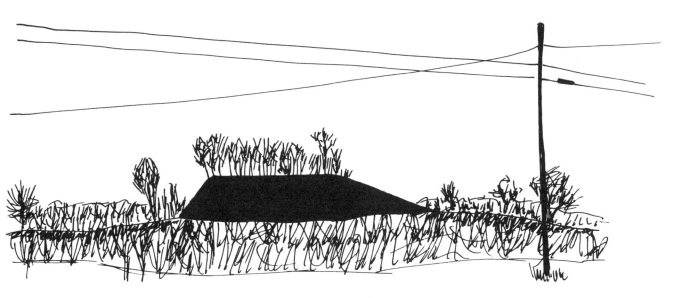

55. The Great Mound of the Great Mound Division—Mound Bottom

defense as its neighbor was. Completely encircled by the Harpeth River on all but the western edge of the village, it had the additional protection of lying at the base of high, perpendicular cliffs beyond the river on its northern and eastern sides. Hence, the only naturally unprotected side was to the west and this was the direction in which the town linked up with the Great Mound town.

A large pyramidal mound surrounded by several smaller mounds, all situated on a broad plaza, made up this town. Living sites were located to the south of the large mound. The entrance to this town was on the south side of the narrow piece of land formed by the bend of the river. It consisted of a series of earthworks through which a passage probably existed at one time.

The entire area of the Mound Bottom Division is still visible today, much as it was at its zenith, with the exception of course of the buildings. The road leading to it lies to the north of Highway 70 and branches from the highway just east of the bridge crossing the Harpeth. The road follows the bend of the river, so that in winter when the leaves are off the trees, the viewer can get a very good look at the entire village from three sides.

The question as to the events which fell upon all of these people to cause them to disappear remains as elusive and unanswered to us as the same question did when presented with the Old Town evidence. The folks who made Mound Bottom, including both divisions, their home were most likely of the same group of people who lived at Old Town, Fewkes, and all the other prehistoric sites that we have surveyed in this book. They belonged to the Mississippian Period of culture, which it will be recalled was most noted for the construction of temple mounds. Both the Great Mound and its division and the large mound in the Mound Bottom Division are huge temple mounds and reflective of the style of mound construction of the period. Being allied to the other people of the Harpeth River Valley, they probably shared the same fate; i.e., assimilation into other peoples' culture by gradual blending rather than outright conquest. On the other hand, we have the evidence found by Myer in the Great Mound Division that fire was responsible for much destruction at this site. Perhaps a mighty conquerer did come to this place as described earlier and laid waste to the entire village. Perhaps these conquerers carried off with them whatever survivors remained. Who knows? The only thing we know for sure is best expressed in the report of the 1923 expedition to the area. In its closing statements it says:

> "Beyond all question the town has been destroyed long before the coming of the whites. In like manner the Indians living in this section when the whites arrived stated their ancestors had also found these vestiges of some unknown people lying silent and deserted along this beautiful river when they came into this region."

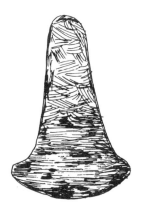

Epilogue

In the "Preface" to this book I expressed apprehension at the rapid destruction of buildings, bridges, etc. that are so much a part of our early heritage. In an age when highway construction and urban renewal are pulling down many old homes and buildings, and the urgency of education is bringing about newer, more efficient facilities for children, many old landmarks in city and country are rapidly disappearing. In the city, old buildings make way for inner city loops in the Interstate Highway System or else are removed in order to raise new structures more pleasing to our suddenly achieved critical eyes. In the country, improved roads can no longer be supported by the old one lane iron bridges that served horse, foot, carriage, and early automobile traffic for so many faithful years. So the old bridges come down and modern, concrete two lane structures go up in their places.

The general store is gone. Today, when everyone has transportation that can get them many miles in just a few minutes, it is easier to trade at the giant supermarkets that have sprouted up all over the countryside in city and in country alike than to trade with stores having limited stocks. There was a time when a family could get everything it needed either off of the farm or at the general store. This is no longer true. With the thousands of commodities of every thinkable shape, form, and fashion that are present on today's market, there is no earthly way that a small store can satisfy everyone's desires.

There is no need for blacksmiths anymore since everyone has a tractor. Consequently, it is a rare thing indeed to find a smith's shop in this day and time. The same is true for mills. Why grind corn all day when you can buy it "ready made" at the store?

Even the churches have given in to this "new sophistication". Scattered across the country are many one room churches that stand deserted, rotting away until they are mercifully razed. Newer, nicer structures have replaced these old log and wooden frame buildings, and the joyful singing that you used to hear on a summer Sunday morning bursting through the open windows and doors of these tiny churches is now all bottled up in the brick and the cement and the plaster of the modern version of God's House.

It isn't too late to still see many of these old structures that link us to our frontier heritage. But you won't see them in their prime, because now they lay deserted. No more do children in their flour sack dresses and corduroy pants play outside the old school house, dreading the sound of the "ding-dong" of the bell calling them back in for resumption of their studies. No more do you hear the hammer of the smith as he merrily goes about his life's work. Maybe some of us live too much in the past, but I know that I miss these things, and it disturbs me that what few of these places are left are themselves going rapidly. The day is shortly coming when our country will be typically modern, with none of the remembrances of the old days left.

In rambling about the countryside gathering information for this book, I came across many of these old churches, schools, and stores, most of them deserted. I came across a lot of the old bridges, too, and ironically most of them are still in use though the majority have had new road beds placed across them. Some of these structures I could locate history on and others I could not.

Scattered throughout this book are the sketches that I have made of all these places. It is hoped that perhaps among these sketches, there may be one recognizable to a reader and that his memory may be returned to the nostalgic days of his youth. These places will be gone before too much longer. Hopefully, some of their glory and "good times" can be preserved, if not in fact, at least in print.

Selected
Bibliography

Corbin, Diana Fontaine Maury. *A Life of Matthew Fontaine Maury*. London, Samson Low, Marston, Seartle and Rivington, 1888. 326 pp. A very informative book about this great American, compiled by his daughter.

Daniels, Jonathan. *The Devil's Backbone*. New York, McGraw-Hill Book Co. Inc., 1962. 278 pp. One of the fine "American Trail Series," edited by A. B. Guthere, Jr. Deals with the history of the Natchez Trace.

Estes, P. M. "Historic Places in Davidson, Williamson, Maury, and Giles Counties," Nashville, Nashville Auto Club, 192?. 29 pp. A small but informative pamphlet describing much of the history of the included counties.

Hicks, Edward P. "Origin of the Name Harpeth" in American Historical Magazine, Vol. V, Number 2, Nashville, Peabody Normal College, 1900. A brief treatise on the possible origins of the name Harpeth, particularly the "Spectator" theory.

Jones, Joseph. *Explorations of the Aboriginal Remains of Tennessee*, Washington, D.C., The Smithsonian Institution, 1876. Reprinted in 1970 by the Tenase Co., Knoxville. 171 pp. A "must" volume on early archaeology of Tennessee.

Lewis, T.M.N. and Kneberg, Madeline. *Tribes That Slumber*. Knoxville, The University of Tennessee, 1958, 196 pp. A very good introduction to pre-historic life in Tennessee.

Thurston, Gates P. *The Antiquities of Tennessee*. Cincinnati, The Robert Clarke Co., 1897. Reprinted in 1964 by Tenase Explorers, Knoxville. 360 pp. Another of the "must" volumes on early archaeology of Tennessee.

Wellman, Paul I. *Spawn of Evil*. New York, Doubleday and Co., Inc., 1964, 350 pp. A history of outlaws and their deeds in the old Southwest. Contains quite a bit of information on the Harpe Brothers, John A. Murrell, and the Natchez Trace.

INDEX

PRODUCTION & PRINTING CREDITS

Typography by Modern Typographers, Inc.
Type face used in this book 10 point Times Roman
Book designed by Lewis Bradley Whitfield
Indexing by Sarah M. Whitfield

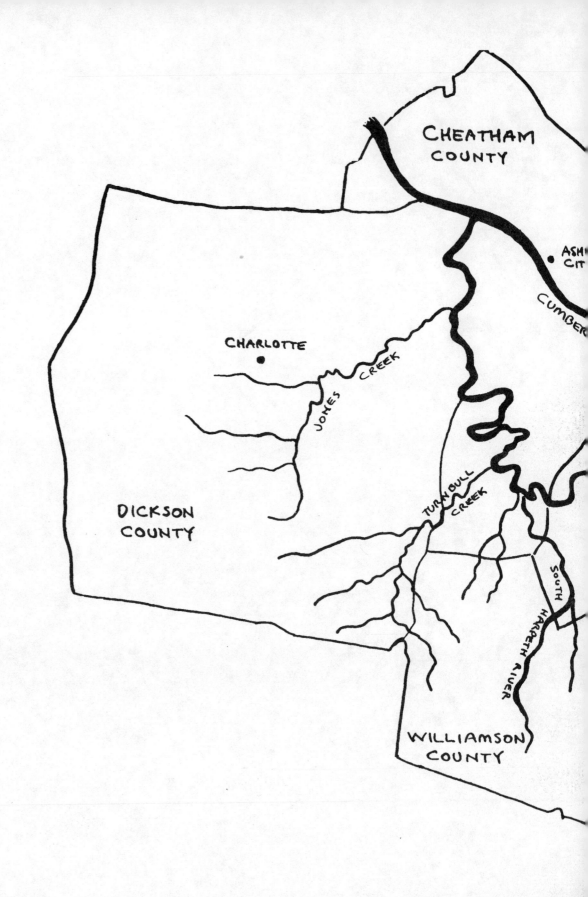

CHEATHAM
COUNTY

ASH
CIT

CUMBER

CHARLOTTE

JONES CREEK

TURNBULL CREEK

DICKSON
COUNTY

SOUTH HARPETH RIVER

WILLIAMSON
COUNTY

The Harpeth